Sexual Integrity

Sexual Integrity

The Answer to AIDS

JACK DOMINIAN

Darton, Longman and Todd
London

First published in 1987 by
Darton, Longman and Todd Ltd
89 Lillie Road, London SW6 1UD

Reprinted 1988 (twice)

© 1987 Jack Dominian

ISBN 0 232 51750 9

British Library Cataloguing in Publication Data

Dominian, Jack
    Sexual integrity : the answer to AIDS.
    1. Sex
    I. Title
    306.7   HQ21

    ISBN 0–232–51750–9

Phototypeset by
Input Typesetting Ltd
London SW19 8DR
Printed and bound in Great Britain by
Anchor Brendon Ltd
Tiptree, Essex

Contents

Acknowledgements

Scriptural quotations are taken from the New Jerusalem Bible published and copyright 1985 by Darton, Longman and Todd Ltd and Doubleday & Co. Inc. and used by permission of the publishers.

Introduction

The arrival of AIDS has created a new sexual situation in many societies. The previous world-wide phenomenon which affected sexual behaviour was the advent of the contraceptive pill some twenty-five years ago. Widespread contraception heralded a new era for sexual morals: sexual intercourse could then be pursued for its pleasure-giving qualities and its other values were relegated to a secondary place.

Christianity has faced this sexual revolution with mixed feelings. It knows that the rampant neglect of pre- and intra-marital chastity is damaging to human beings but its voice has not been heard: too many people interpret this teaching as a mere extension of a negative attitude to sexuality; too many have seen the churches as annihilators of sexual joy. But the problems of Christianity have not ended with the hostility entertained against its teachings. The churches have been faced with an additional problem, namely that the very basis of their traditional sexual teaching has undergone a profound revolution.

For over three thousand years the Judaeo-Christian tradition has based its sexual morality on the link between intercourse and procreation. But the advent of widespread and reliable contraception has now severed this link. Although contraceptive techniques have been recorded since Egyptian times the complete and effective separation between coitus and procreation has only been effected in the last quarter of a century. The impact of this revolution has been gigantic, and the Christian churches were faced with an enormous challenge to produce an alternative basis for sexual

1

morality and theology. Such a development has yet to emerge clearly and its absence is a tremendous handicap to asserting the Christian position authoritatively. Indeed the Roman Catholic Church has refused to accept this break between coitus and procreation, although – like everyone else – it accepts birth regulation.

Thus the arrival of AIDS, with its demands for a change in moral behaviour, has coincided with a period of radical transition in the very foundations of Christian understanding of the meaning of human sexuality. People will interpret the AIDS epidemic in a variety of ways. For example, for those who believe in a God who never ceases to dialogue with his people created out of love, the arrival of AIDS must be seen as carrying profound meaning. Then there are some who see this disease as a punishment for ignoring God's laws, although the overwhelming majority of Christians do not interpret the matter in this way.

Apart from the opportunities offered to show care and concern to those affected with the disease, AIDS can become an occasion to examine afresh the meaning of sexuality. It is an opportunity to reformulate the basis of sexual morality in the light of the traditional link between intercourse and procreation that has now come under pronounced human control: for the majority of men and women the connection has been suppressed through contraception or another form of effective birth regulation. A new era has arrived in which there is a pronounced shift in sexuality from biology to personal love.

This book aims to chart, against the background of AIDS, the movement of sexuality from an emphasis on biology to that of personal love: I shall attempt to show that the traditional beliefs held by Christians in sexual matters are still valid, but that their effective pursuit needs a major shift in the understanding of human sexuality.

This is not however a major treatise on the subject. There are no scientific or theological references and no theme has been treated exhaustively. Its purpose is to alert people to the dire danger of AIDS and to provide a basis for changes in sexual behaviour based on personal love which apply not only to Christians of all denominations but to everybody. For it is my profound belief that such Christian teaching is applicable to all men and women endeavouring to do justice to their integrity. For too long the voice of Christianity on sexual matters has been dismissed as irrelevant. AIDS is now bringing about a rapid transformation in society and once again Christian teaching on sexual matters is being sought. But it is absolutely vital that what this teaching has to say does justice not only to Judaeo-Christian revelation but to the secular reality of sexuality itself. As with all human affairs sexuality is an ever changing secular reality which is taken up and made into a divine mystery. This book attempts to outline this conjunction.

1

AIDS

AIDS stands for acquired immune deficiency syndrome and has been described as the most serious disease in the world today. We have been accustomed in the last twenty-five years to think of infectious diseases as the least harmful problems we have to face. The wide use of antibiotics and the presence of vaccination and immunisation have between them removed some of humanity's worst scourges. Indeed young people have no awareness of the dread their parents experienced of such diseases as tuberculosis and poliomyelitis, both killers in their own right. In the field of sexually transmitted diseases, to which AIDS largely belongs, penicillin and other drugs managed to persuade people that even if they caught syphilis or gonorrhoea a short course of treatment would be sufficient to reverse the effects. We have come to treat infectious diseases with disdain and only rarely has the public been aware of any serious consequences resulting from them. Medicine has concentrated instead on the dangers of cancer and heart disease, the twin conditions that are the main causes of mortality in western society.

No one was prepared for a new and lethal condition. For let there be no doubt about it, AIDS *is* a killer. We know of no treatment that can reverse its destructive characteristics.

In this chapter I will describe the facts as we know them at present. I use the words 'at present' deliberately because there is a great deal we do not know about the disease, and in time new facts will emerge which will add to its complexity. The reasons why so much attention is paid to this condition are that it is a serious risk to life and that its main transmission is sexual. Everyone therefore who participates in sexual activity is potentially liable to be infected. Furthermore only one act of intercourse is needed.

History of the Disease

The first cases of AIDS were reported in the United States in 1981. The disease was detected in homosexual men and initially it was believed to exist only in this group of people. It is now known that this is not the case and that heterosexual men and women are also affected.

The disease is not confined to the USA; indeed apart from spreading to many other parts of the world – including Britain – it has been found that AIDS is epidemic in sub-Saharan Africa and in parts of the western world. In 1985 there were 16,500 cases in the USA, which had risen to 20,305 by the middle of 1986. In Europe 2004 were reported in 1985. In the United Kingdom there were some 362 cases by mid-1986, of which nearly half had died. The increase in numbers is staggering. In 1982 three cases were reported. In 1983 the number reported increased to 28; in 1984 to 77; and in 1985 to 167. The most recent figures show further increases, thus by January 1987, 355 had died of the disease and 686 were suffering from it.

Although it is western nations that are responding with alarm to AIDS it is vital to remember that the central part of Africa is in the midst of a large-scale epidemic. A number of studies from cities in Zaire, Zambia, Kenya and Rwanda show that as many as 5 to 10 per cent of young adults in some urban areas have been infected and that the disease is spreading to rural populations and children. Furthermore unlike western countries the disease in Africa has spread mainly through heterosexual contact. This is important both because of the need for travellers to be particularly careful of sexual behaviour in these African countries, and because Africa may set a precedent of what will happen in other countries.

The Sufferers and the Transmission of AIDS

By the end of May 1986, of the 362 cases of AIDS reported in the United Kingdom 350 were men and 12 women; that is, the overwhelming majority were men, but, in the light of increasing information, unless the disease is contained more women sufferers are likely in the future. Of the 350 men no less than 318 were homosexual or bisexual, and 17 were haemophiliacs; five men and one woman became infected by blood transfusion; and three men and one woman were injecting themselves with drugs in their veins. This list shows that at present those mainly at risk are: people who participate in sexual activity, particularly if they are homosexuals; those who receive blood (haemophiliacs have been particularly vulnerable); and intravenous drug abusers.

It can been seen that homosexual men are most at risk. Research has shown that the passive homosexual man, who participates in anal intercourse and therefore receives semen, is at maximum risk, particularly if he has many partners. It is believed that anything which causes damage to the anus or the rectum adds to the risk. The active sexual partner is at lower risk, but far from immune.

Transmission from infected men to women is now well established and an infected donor can pass the disease to a woman who is artificially inseminated. Female to male transmission has been much less in evidence. But the virus has been found in vaginal and cervical fluids, and as more women become infected – particularly prostitutes – the likelihood is that women will become an increasing source of infection.

After homosexual men, recipients of blood (including haemophiliacs) have been the next largest group infected with AIDS. Before the condition was well known these people had received contaminated blood and caught the disease in that way. This has surely been one of the most cruel acts of fate. However the situation here is improving considerably as blood is now tested before being used for transfusions.

Another source of transmission is by infected syringes and

needles which are shared by those who inject themselves with drugs; these drug abusers are greatly at risk. In one study it has been shown that as many as 85 per cent of an intravenous drug-abusing population may become infected with the virus. This group of young people are a source of considerable anxiety and consideration is now given to supplying sterile syringes and needles to addicts who use the intravenous route. This free availability of sterile syringes poses moral problems in that it may be thought addiction is being supported. Nevertheless the risk of AIDS is so serious that I believe the supply of sterile syringes perfectly justified.

Another mode of transmission is from mother to child. The virus is likely to be passed on while the foetus is in the uterus. Alternatively it may be passed through breast milk or contact with the mother's infected blood. Most rarely, the virus has been passed through the donation of an organ.

On the more positive side, studies have shown that health workers such as doctors, nurses and laboratory staff, who are in contact with AIDS sufferers or their products, are not prone to catch the disease. One study of 1758 such health workers who had been directly or indirectly in contact with patients suffering from AIDS showed that 26 or 1.5 per cent were shown to have the virus antibody in their blood, but 23 of these were homosexual men. In fact only two infected workers had received needle injuries with infected blood. Thus, provided that routine precautions are taken, those who have to take care of AIDS sufferers should have no major worries of contracting the disease.

Another reassuring study examined the risk of transmission of the disease to relatives, children and parents of 39 adults suffering from AIDS. After nearly two years of contact these relatives were shown to be free from the disease, with the exception of one child, a five-year-old girl, who had almost certainly caught the infection after birth from her mother.

In summary we can say that, while the virus has been isolated from blood, semen, vaginal and anal secretions, tears, saliva and breast milk, and may be present in other body fluids including urine, it is presently widely recognised that its main transmission is through sexual intercourse or blood contamination. In this respect contaminated instruments may carry the disease in tattooing and ear piercing. The presence of the virus in saliva poses problems regarding kissing and the receiving of the communion chalice. So far, research suggests that saliva is not a particularly rich source of the virus and at present there is no evidence that either kissing or receiving the communion chalice carries any risk, but the ordinary precautions of wiping the chalice after each communicant has received the wine should be carried out scrupulously.

The Virus and the Disease

The link between AIDS and a virus has already been mentioned. It is almost certain that a retrovirus first isolated in France in 1983 and called 'lymphadenopathy associated virus', or LAV, and a similar one found in the USA in 1984 called 'human T cell lymphotropic virus type III', are the infecting agents. The dates show how recent our knowledge of AIDS is. These two discoveries have been put together and called in medical circles HTLVIII/LAV. Once people have become infected, our present knowledge suggests that they remain infected for life. The person who is infected may not be detected initially, but in a matter of weeks tests can show the presence of the virus in the body.

It should be stressed that not everyone infected with the virus develops the full-blown disease AIDS. Initially, that is, within three weeks of the person being infected, he or she develops flu-like symptoms such as fever, feeling unwell, aches and pains, sweats or sore throat, headaches and an enlargement of glands. After two or three more weeks these symptoms clear up. There follows a period in which the infected person may have no disturbance or may feel unwell, tired, lose weight and have diarrhoea. During this period glands may be enlarged and infection of the skin may be present. But of course the main symptom during this phase is anxiety concerning the possibility of the development of the full-blown disease AIDS.

Finally a variable proportion of persons infected with the virus HTLVIII/LAV develop the acquired immune deficiency syndrome, AIDS, which essentially destroys the body's defences against infection and malignancy and which leads to death. Initially it was found that 9 to 14 per cent of infected homosexual men had developed AIDS when they were followed up over two years. But this evidence of the lethal disease has increased to between 15 and 34 per cent over a three-year period.

Counselling

Since there is no cure for the full-blown disease and there appears to be none in sight in the immediate future, the approach to this infection is twofold; that of counselling and prevention. In this section I will deal with counselling. First there are the numerous men and women who are worried in case they are infected. Care should be taken to ensure that there is real cause for anxiety and that the fear is not part of a wider anxiety problem. The possibility of infection must be taken into account and if no evidence exists reassurance is appropriate. By reassurance I do not mean the dismissal of the fear but a considerate response, given the person's circumstances and background.

If the person has genuine reasons to fear infection then an appropriate test can be done, taking due precaution regarding the time factor for positive results to show. Testing immediately after sexual activity may not be conclusive one way or another, as we have seen that it may take two to three months to show a positive result.

At some stage before a test, or after (if it is positive), the impact on others must be considered. Relatives and friends are a priority. How does one reveal to a friend who may be a lover that one is being investigated for such a condition? If the person undergoing a test is a homosexual and his relatives are not aware of the situation, both will need help with the revelation and coming to terms with the sexual orientation. A wife may be shocked to discover that her husband has homosexual tendencies, has had an extramarital affair, or has been with a prostitute. Everyone concerned needs help in coming to terms with their fears, anger, prejudice and the risk of catching the infection. The suspect can be tormented by the anxieties of shame, guilt and rejection.

The person who is infected has to live with the whole range of emotions from fear of developing the full-blown disease to the embarrassment of finding themselves in that predicament. He or she must be seen regularly, monitored physically and encouraged about his/her prospects of survival. These men and women have to come to terms with their own inner feelings and those of others and need an enormous amount of support. The anxiety of being an outcast has been known since the beginning of time and this virus has reawakened that plight in those who are afflicted.

Secondly there are those with the disease itself. People who develop AIDS know they are destined to die within two years. As in all circumstances where lethal disease strikes there are the physical, psychological and spiritual aspects of care. The patient must be treated as actively as possible so that the best quality of life is maintained. Above all, every effort should be made to render the meaning of life significant. In spiritual terms it is vital to make the patient feel acknowledged and accepted and loved as a person received by both man and God unconditionally.

Prevention

Prevention remains the best and only 'cure' we have at the present time. Since the infection is most commonly transmitted sexually the best form of prevention is to confine sexual intercourse to one partner within marriage. The whole of this book will examine the implications of such an attitude which is familiar to the Christian and other religions but has become unfashionable in recent times.

Pre- and intramarital chastity has long been advocated by

the whole Judaeo-Christian tradition, with variable success. In terms of the risk of AIDS, complete continence is obviously the ideal. If this is not followed then sexual contact should not be promiscuous as the greater the number of partners the greater the risk of becoming infected. And finally, if sexual intercourse does take place, then it is advised that a condom be used. This latter recommendation has caused confusion in Roman Catholic circles but in reality the matter is very simple. When a condom is used as a protection against the virus of AIDS its main purpose is to prevent the infection, not to avoid conception. It is vital that everyone should take precautions against such a dreadful possibility as AIDS. In particular the person who is infected and who continues to have sex should ensure that the disease does not spread. Anal sex is particularly risky and should be avoided. Ejaculation in the mouth should also be avoided.

As regards becoming infected through blood: although blood for transfusion is tested and the appropriate treatment carried out, still the utmost care should be exercised. Intravenous drug users must be particularly careful about the needles and syringes they use as this will hopefully avoid infection by contamination.

But as infection spreads to women and the sexual route is the main source of transmission, so it is that sexual education is the vital key to prevention.

Compassion to the Sufferer

Everyone, but particularly the Christian community, has a duty to show love and compassion to the infected and those with the disease. We need to ensure that the infected person remains our spouse or friend, colleague or employee. We must not stigmatise such a person and make them the new 'leper' of our age. We have to help them come to terms with themselves and let them ventilate their feelings. Disgust is an easily mobilised feeling which has to be suppressed. In this country so many infected people are homosexual and the combination of homosexuality and venereal disease can become dynamite.

11

Acceptance, friendship and communication have to be the hallmarks of all those who relate to the infected and must be extended to the victims of AIDS. These men, and in the future women, have to be helped to run their lives normally for as long as they can. It has been shown that relatives of AIDS victims are not particularly exposed to the risk of catching the disease and the support of the community should be aimed at reconciling the victim with his or her family.

When the person is acutely ill he or she should be nursed and assisted as any other sick person. We should pray for them and avoid at all costs the feeling that they deserve their affliction.

To do all the positive things that responsibility and love demand means overcoming ignorance and powerful feelings of fear and disgust. Most people immunise themselves from their anxieties by believing that the worst will never happen to them. Nobody believes that *they* will become victims of cancer or suffer heart disease. Few people can ever imagine that *they* will become infected with the virus of AIDS. The startling fact is that anyone who has sexual intercourse with a partner whose background is unknown is at risk. The publicity given by the media and the government to this issue is of great importance in making everybody think twice about casual sex.

Furthermore it is vital that we look at our feelings of fear and disgust whenever we have to relate to someone who is infected or has the full-blown disease. In practice the risk of becoming infected by them is remote. We should encourage our normal concern, care and compassion to have full expression. Those who are infected and sick need our friendship, our support and our practical help. In particular, Christians should act with love and compassion. Professional help can allay anxiety but it is the ordinary man and woman who is needed to befriend, to do the shopping for those incapacitated, to reconcile victims with their relatives and to ensure that in the end the AIDS victim has a dignified death.

God Speaking

The arrival of AIDS has brought a spate of remarks about God's intentions in allowing this disease, with all its devastation, to spread throughout the world. There are those who see AIDS as God's judgment on a rebellious and salacious world. In particular, the homosexual community has been subjected to severe diatribes. Others see the disease as an opportunity to reassert traditional morality at a stroke.

Those who see in AIDS God's judgment on a world gone mad over sex are often authoritarian punitive figures who seek an opportunity to control human behaviour through fear and retribution. Such men and women have always existed and seize any opportunity to propagate their views. But Christianity must always seek to reflect the personality of Christ in its reflections on God's dialogue with mankind. This dialogue was brought to perfection in the incarnation when God took on the fullness of being human. Jesus showed us that love and compassion are the principal means of responding to our neighbour; at the same time he raised human integrity to an unprecedented level of perfection. Each successive generation has to exercise love and compassion and realise a little bit more of the kingdom of God. And this is precisely what I believe AIDS is meant to achieve: on the one hand we have to expend a tremendous amount of care towards all who are infected or have the full-blown disease, and on the other we have to review the meaning of sexuality in terms of human integrity. Both the world and the churches have to learn from this new situation. The reassessment has to be carried out in faith and trust that God is speaking to us, as he has always done, and yet he does not want to evoke in us a fear response. St John the evangelist, who has more to say about love than anyone else, has written in his first epistle: 'In love there is no room for fear, but perfect love drives out fear, because fear implies punishment and whoever is afraid has not come to perfection in love' (1 John 4:18).

This reassessment is long overdue in Christian circles. For nearly a quarter of a century there have been large-scale sexual changes which have taken Christianity unawares. For over three thousand years the link between sex and procreation controlled all thinking, but now this link is broken and has been coupled with an attitude to sexuality where the pleasure motive dominates. Christians who bemoaned the permissive society were not in a position to influence it because of their reluctance to realise that, as mankind learns increasingly to control biology, human behaviour can change. The real challenge is to have such trust in God's wisdom as to be sure that, no matter what change takes place, the basic values that Judaeo-Christianity has revealed will remain viable even if mankind learns the secrets of how sexuality operates. It is inevitable that men and women will learn to control their environment and themselves. It is the task of Christianity to respect mankind's autonomy and yet, at the same time, to assert and reassert the fundamentals that cannot be overthrown. These fundamentals relate to the revelation that man was created in the image of God (Gen. 1:27) and that God is love (1 John 4:8). So that personal love is the ultimate criterion by which all human behaviour has to be assessed. For too long Christianity has relied too heavily on biology for its sexual thinking. The time is now appropriate to move from biology to person and love and I believe AIDS is God's way of acknowledging this transformation.

2

Homosexuality and AIDS

In Chapter 1 it is shown that homosexual men have, so far, formed a large proportion of those who have become infected with the HTLVIII/LAV virus. The pre-eminence of homosexual men has invited some fairly virulent remarks about these people and, implicitly, their sexual activity.

There is no doubt that since the overwhelming majority of human beings are orientated heterosexually, get married and have families, the orientation and sexual behaviour of homosexual men and women are likely to stir up various feelings including curiosity, fear, hostility and disgust. It is well established by psychology that we protect ourselves from whatever frightens or threatens us by casting aspersions on it, by ridicule or attack. Thus homosexuals of both sexes, but particularly men, are a small minority who are subject, like all minorities, to oppression, contempt and hostility. This hostility ranges from denying such people jobs, discriminating against them in promotion, denying them accommodation and treating them as a fringe group with no rights and no entitlement to be heard.

It is not surprising against such hostility that homosexuals tend to band themselves together, visit their own centres of recreation, are secretive, indulge in fleeting relationships and engage in promiscuous sexual activity. Such activity among men may involve anal intercourse which can arouse feelings of disgust. It is often forgotten that anal intercourse is not confined to homosexual men but is practised between men and women, although it is illegal even in the married. Indeed all orifices of the body can be and are used for sexual activity.

15

Anal intercourse has undoubtedly been a common route for the spread of the HTLVIII/LAV virus and has fired the imagination for vitriolic attacks against homosexuals. Such overt hostility represents the ugly aspect of society and it is particularly contemptible when it is supported on moral or religious grounds. Christianity must reassert that everybody is created in the image of God and as such is entitled to be treated with equal care, compassion and justice, and this applies to homosexuals as much as to anyone else.

But in addition to these ordinary anxieties a number of fantasies exist about homosexuals. They are believed to dress differently, and to speak and behave in effeminate ways. Above all every homosexual who assaults a boy sexually is treated in such a way that it is easy to deduce that all homosexuals seduce children. In fact, although there are exceptions, the vast majority of homosexual men cannot be differentiated from their heterosexual counterparts in intelligence, education, work, dress or habits, apart from their emotional and sexual inclinations. Above all, the homosexual adult who molests children sexually is in a very rare minority. Heterosexual abuse of children is more common in terms of absolute numbers. In general it can be said that homosexual men and women are as law-abiding, useful, creative and artistic members of society as heterosexuals. It is only fear and prejudice that makes us hold these suspicions against them. Anyone who has worked closely with homosexual people knows from first-hand experience that they are as fully accomplished as their heterosexual colleagues. But the stigma and prejudice remain and AIDS risks the possibility of a new flare up of this very old tendency.

The Incidence and Cause of Homosexuality

The best study of the incidence of homosexuality is probably that of A. C. Kinsey *et al.*, *Sexual Behaviour in the Human Male*, published over forty years ago, showing that among males 37 per cent had some homosexual contact to the point of orgasm between adolescence and old age; 13 per cent of men had more of the homosexual contact than the heterosexual for at least three years between the ages of fifteen and fifty-five and 8 per cent of men were exclusively homosexual for at least three years between sixteen and fifty-five. Finally 4 per cent of men are exclusively homosexual throughout their lives after the onset of adolescence. These figures tend to suggest that male homosexuality is a condition representing a spectrum rather than a sharp division from heterosexuality. It is important to note again that heterosexually-orientated married males who indulge in homosexual activity can become infected with the AIDS virus and then pass it on to their wives.

The incidence of homosexuality in women is much smaller. One of the differences found by Kinsey is that women are more faithful, whereas men have many more partners. This tendency for homosexual men to be more promiscuous has been a contributing factor in spreading the HTLVIII/LAV virus. Nevertheless the fact that some homosexual men are promiscuous does not mean they all are; but it does mean that those who are have few committed relationships, are more likely to be isolated and lonely and, if they become ill from AIDS, need a great deal of support in their vulnerable predicament.

The much larger incidence of men who have had some homosexual experience in their life against those who are exclusively homosexual should suggest great caution in labelling anyone homosexual. In particular, adolescents may go through phases of being homosexually attracted and emerge to form stable heterosexual relationships. It is dangerous to reach hasty conclusions about the sexual orientation of anyone before the middle twenties.

Even though the exclusive homosexual is a distinct minority, he or she does represent millions of men and women across the world, and the overall numbers do present an important social and moral problem.

Homosexual behaviour has been known since ancient times and, as we shall see, has been condemned in the Judaeo-Christian tradition. One would have thought that by now we would know and understand what factors contribute to it; but we do not. Since the time of Freud there have been dynamic psychological theories which try to explain its presence and their protagonists appear certain that homosexuality is caused by faulty sexual development in relation to the parents. Others deny these explanations and suggest that physical factors contribute to homosexuality. Controversy abounds and the debate is heated. Vogues of treatment come and go but there is no generally acknowledged way of reversing homosexual trends. Indeed when the social, legal and moral pressures recede most exclusive homosexuals have no wish to change their orientation and so the moral dilemma about their state continues.

Homosexuality and Christianity

There is little doubt that western society has been influenced by the Judaeo-Christian tradition and the law has reflected the hostility of this tradition to homosexuality. The position in Christian circles varies from strongly upholding the orthodox criticism of homosexuality, to examining the reasons for wanting to alter this position. The Roman Catholic Church upholds the traditional position of seeing homosexual actions as 'intrinsically disordered'. In a letter to the bishops of the Catholic Church in November 1986 the Congregation of the Doctrine of the Faith expressed the clearest and unequivocal condemnation of homosexuality in the following terms:

> Although the particular inclination of the homosexual person is not a sin, it is a more or less strong tendency ordered towards an intrinsic moral evil, and thus the inclination itself must be seen as an objective disorder. Therefore special concern and pastoral attention should be directed towards those who have this condition, lest they be led to believe that the living out of this orientation in homosexual activity is a morally acceptable option. It is not.

This is brief, to the point and unequivocal. On what grounds

18

is it taught? As in all moral matters in the Roman Catholic Church its teaching is based on reason, which is variously expressed as the natural law, scriptures and tradition.

As far as reason is concerned, human sexuality is seen fashioned in a complementarity of male and female, designed to come together in marriage in order to transmit life. Here the connection between the sexual act and biology is paramount. Homosexual acts are not open to life and therefore are 'intrinsically disordered'. In other words the sexual activity of the homosexual is such that an essential component of its potential, hitherto considered the essential characteristic, is seen as missing. The intrinsic disorder is, of course, more than the inability to have children, but rather it is the male-female complementarity which is missing.

After this basic call to reason the teaching moves to the scriptures. A fundamental view is taken that God in his infinite wisdom and love has fashioned mankind into male and female, designed for a complementarity which reflects the inner unity of God himself. This complementarity expresses itself in a striking way in transmitting life by mutual donation of self to the other. And then there follow a series of texts which condemn homosexuality.

The first is the story of the destruction of Sodom, from Genesis:

When the two angels reached Sodom in the evening, Lot was sitting at the gate of Sodom. As soon as Lot saw them, he stood up to greet them, and bowed to the ground. 'My lords,' he said, 'please come down to your servant's house to stay the night and wash your feet. Then you can make an early start on your journey.' 'No,' they said, 'we shall spend the night in the square.' But he pressed them so much that they went home with him and entered his house. He prepared a meal for them, baking unleavened bread, and they had supper.

They had not gone to bed when the house was surrounded by the townspeople, the men of Sodom both young and old, all the people without exception. Calling

19

out to Lot they said, 'Where are the men who came to you tonight? Send them out to us so that we can have intercourse with them.' (Gen. 19:1–5)

The story goes on to tell how Lot offered his two virgin daughters instead but the people insisted on their original demand. The two angels thwarted the men's efforts, protected Lot and his family and ultimately God destroyed Sodom and Gomorrah. This is considered the classical text against homosexuality.

In Leviticus the conditions for belonging to the Chosen People are described and homosexuality is proscribed. In Leviticus 18:22 we find: 'You will not have intercourse with a man as you would with a woman. This is a hateful thing.' Again in Leviticus 20:13 the injunction is maintained: 'The man who has intercourse with a man in the same way as with a woman: they have done a hateful thing together; they will be put to death; their blood will be on their own heads.'

In the New Testament St Paul continues the condemnation. In 1 Corinthians 6:9 he lists homosexuals as those who will not inherit the kingdom of God: 'Make no mistake – the sexually immoral, idolaters, adulterers, the self-indulgent, sodomites, thieves, misers, drunkards, slanderers and swindlers, none of these will inherit the kingdom of God.' Those who oppose the church's teaching are quick to remind us that the church takes a particularly hostile view towards sexual offences but by comparison is indulgent to the other categories of St Paul. In particular it is much kinder to alcoholics, a problem which prevails among many Catholics and a number of its priests.

In Romans Paul confronts the pagan world and compares it with Christianity. In this comparison he cites homosexuality as an example of the pagan degeneration.

That is why God abandoned them to degrading passions: why their women have exchanged natural intercourse for unnatural practices; and the men, in a similar fashion, too, giving up normal relations with women, are consumed with passion for each other, men doing shameful things with men and receiving in themselves due reward for their perversion. (Rom. 1:26–27).

There is a further attack against homosexuality in Timothy (1 Tim 1:10).

Thus the Roman Catholic Church bases its condemnation of homosexuality on a combination of natural law and the scriptures. Other Christians, who do not rely on natural law, predominantly use the scriptures for their disapproval.

What can be said in favour of the view that homosexual behaviour should not be condemned?

To start with there is a general feeling that being a homosexual is a state which is no fault of their own and the denial of sexual activity appears to be a massive assault on a meaningful activity, an attitude of basic injustice, which is contrary to the overall teaching of Christianity, which should be based on love. In fact homosexuals feel that the condemnation of their overt sexuality is a gross injustice and a violation of love. Many Christians are torn between their basic feelings of unease about homosexuality and their desire to exercise an attitude of love. The teaching on homosexuality seems harsh and in contrast to Jesus befriending minorities, fringe groups and the outcasts. The orthodox answer has been that the homosexual person must be treated with dignity, care and compassion but must not be encouraged to indulge in homosexual acts. The reply to this is that to ask all homosexuals to live a life of celibacy is an intolerable burden.

What can be said in favour of homosexuality? Let us look at the arguments derived from natural law, based on reason.

It is abundantly clear that the overwhelming majority of mankind is heterosexual and designed for complementarity based on mutual availability. But this is not the ultimate criterion of judging creation. Beyond maleness and femaleness are to be found *persons* and it is the relationship of persons that matters. In the depths of Christian revelation men and women are created in the image of God, but this is a Trinitarian God composed of three persons relating in love to each other. Thus the key of being human is person, relationship

21

and love. The undue emphasis on creativity is based on biology, which is a remote reflection of the total creativity of the whole person.

In the Roman Catholic tradition in particular it should be emphasised that the single state dedicated to God has received extensive attention, and the celibate priest and nun are considered in high esteem. These priests and nuns are nevertheless sexual persons living in relations of love with others. An undue emphasis on the procreative biological component of sexuality distorts the authentic meaning of sexuality. Furthermore within the Roman Catholic tradition marriages are still considered valid even if procreation is not possible. But a final point of immense consideration, which is rarely mentioned, is that Jesus Christ himself points the way to a state beyond marriage and to the fullness of personhood. In the resurrection there will be no marriage. At the heart of sexuality is not the biological dimension but the personal. Our Lord says, 'For when they rise from the dead, men and women do not marry; no, they are like the angels in heaven' (Mark 12:25).

In other words the major argument against homosexuality derived from natural law and based on reason must be the psychological deficiencies of the homosexual, not his or her biological limitations. But in this respect they need to be seen as wounded persons, just as many heterosexual persons are wounded: what need to be encouraged are homosexual relations that are healing.

So much for the rational argument. What about the scriptures? In general it can be said that scriptural statements reflect the knowledge of the time and were written within the limitations of socio-cultural factors. Thus the broad and detailed spectrum of homosexuality to heterosexuality, via bisexuality, is a modern recognition of the complexity of human sexuality. As far as homosexuality is concerned, biblical writers accepted that heterosexuality was the norm and that genital activity should reflect this. In other words homosexual genital acts reflected the choice of people who would be considered to have the *freedom* of heterosexuality and who would thus deliberately indulge in homosexual lust. Furthermore in the case of Paul, his letters were addressed to specific audiences; nowadays we have to *interpret* his letters, including his moral instructions. Take for example his teaching in Corinthians on women in assemblies:

> As in all the churches of God's holy people, women are to remain quiet in the assemblies, since they have no permission to speak: theirs is a subordinate part, as the Law itself says. If there is anything they want to know, they should ask their husbands at home: it is shameful for a woman to speak in the assembly. (1 Cor. 14:34–35).

Our whole attitude to women is fundamentally different from the time of Paul.

Let us now look at the individual texts. As far as the city of Sodom is concerned, the classical Old Testament text against homosexuality, it is strange that this should be its main interpretation. Even in other Old Testament writings different interpretations were taken. Thus Ezekiel suggests that the crimes of Sodom were pride, gluttony, arrogance and complacency and that they never helped the poor and needy. They were proud and engaged in loathsome practices (Ezek. 16:49–50). For Jeremiah their fault was adultery, persistent lying and the refusal to repent (Jer. 23:14). The Wisdom literature refers to the evils of Sodom as inhospitality (Wisd. 19:13–14). Ecclesiasticus thinks that their sin was pride (Ecclus 16:8). Even more relevant, Jesus refers to Sodom in the context of instructions to his apostles to visit towns and preach the good news. If they were not received with hospitality, Jesus tells them:

> Go out into its streets and say, 'We wipe off the very dust of your town that clings to our feet, and leave it with you. Yet be sure of this: the kingdom of God is very near.' I tell you, on the great Day it will be more bearable for Sodom than for that town. (Luke 10:10–12)

It seems from these quotations that Sodom was depicted as

a prototype of evil, with its manifold manifestations, rather than specifically homosexuality.

With regard to the texts in Leviticus, they are part of the Holiness Code, that is, the code containing instructions in culture and ritual, matters that would differentiate the people of Israel from their neighbouring tribes. The specific reference to homosexuality in cultic purity refers to male and female prostitution in temples housing the gods of fertility who were worshipped by surrounding religions. The Israelites judged male prostitution severely because of its connection with these fertility rites of the Canaanites. So the prohibition in Leviticus might have nothing to do with homosexuality and a lot to do with idolatry.

In the New Testament Paul is the primary condemner of homosexual behaviour. Jesus Christ does not mention the matter. As already stated, in Corinthians Paul lists the people who will not inherit the kingdom and these include those who practise homosexual acts. It has been suggested that the Greek words in the text have a variety of meanings including the whole range of sexual immorality, and that the nature of the actions condemned is not precise. Another interpretation is that Paul was primarily concerned with rebellion against the Creator and his creation, with lust and with sexual exploitation, all of which condemnations have stood the test of time. But that does not necessarily include faithful committed homosexual relations. Scholars who have tried to interpret Paul make the point that the distinction between homosexual orientation and genital acts was foreign to his thought world. Paul condemned all homosexual behaviour as wrong and it may be that, if he was aware of the difference between orientation and genital activity, he might have taken a different view of those who have no freedom to choose.

In conclusion it can be said that, although the scriptural texts carry authority with them, they are nowhere as precise as they are made out to be. Indeed a combination of doubts about the rational basis of condemnation coupled with uncertainty about the texts makes a final unequivocal answer difficult to reach. And this, incidentally, applies to other

24

moral matters. Only authoritarian figures admit to no uncertainty.

Where does that leave the Christian community? In terms of teaching, each church reaches its own conclusions. It is vital that Christians should be aware of the teaching of their own particular community. Thus Roman Catholics should be aware of the traditional condemnation of homosexual genital activity, although the homosexual orientation is not sinful. But ultimately the behaviour of the individual must be an expression of his or her own conscience. It is emphasised that this should be an informed conscience which does not lightly reject the teaching of the church. For Roman Catholics the teaching authority of the church must be taken seriously, but it is vital to remember that this teaching is not an infallible one. There is room for legitimate dissent: but dissent must not be made without extreme care.

Nevertheless within the overall traditional condemnation of homosexuality, there is much that can be said and done which softens the rejection of homosexuality. For although it is perfectly true that no church rejects homosexual men and women, the hostile attitude to their behaviour makes them feel condemned and isolated.

First it must be reiterated that, although statistically homosexuality is a distinct minority, it does involve millions of men and women and, whatever our feelings towards them, in practice we have to welcome them as our brothers and sisters in Christ. We find this hard to do. Prejudices rise to the surface and often we seek to avoid them. We do not realise that unconsciously we find them threatening, as we do all people who differ substantially from us. It is important that the Christian community befriends homosexuals and ensures that they do not remain isolated and subject to derision, criticism and violent attacks. Thus parish priests should welcome homosexuals to their churches and, if a group of them emerges, should have the courage of their Christian convictions to allow them to meet within the precincts of the Christian community. It is also vital that preaching on the subject of homosexuality should take place. Like so many

25

sexual subjects, churches appear to speak only when condemnation is mentioned. There is a need to overcome the fears of heterosexuals about their homosexual brethren. Homosexuals need to feel accepted and their problems to be taken seriously. Otherwise all that happens is that homosexuals congregate together and have no one to turn to except each other. They need to be integrated within the Christian community and that is something that has not happened yet.

The next consideration must be given to the lifestyle of homosexual persons. Here it is important to emphasise something about which I feel very strongly, namely that homosexual men and women need a loving relationship as much as their heterosexual counterparts. Homosexuals are persons who need to relate, interact, trust, give and receive affection, concern, understanding, forgiveness and be made to feel lovable.

This means that we should encourage homosexuals to seek one-to-one relationships. Lesbians achieve this very much better than their male counterparts. In my opinion this should be one of the main thrusts of counselling, making it possible to establish long-term stable, loving, faithful, committed relationships. In terms of AIDS the formation of such attachments reduces considerably the risk of multiple sexual liaisons with the increased risks of transmitting the virus. Some might say that encouraging such a relationship would foster sexual activity but my answer is that the formation of a stable loving bond is the most mature form of living, within which a gradual attempt at celibacy can be attempted. Within the context of such stable relationships love, as expressed in sustaining, healing and growth, can take place. For many male homosexuals the effort to form and sustain a stable relationship can be the most vigorous effort towards maturity, wholeness and holiness. In other words I would like to switch the major pastoral effort towards stable relationship. I have no doubt about this, which, incidentally, will be the single most important contribution against the transmission of the virus.

While I am strongly advocating stable personal relationships, I cannot accept the propositions of those who want to call these relationships 'marriages'. The term marriage applies clearly to a man-woman relationship, orientated to such complementarity, with the formation of a family and the continuation of life. I am strongly opposed to the fertilisation of lesbians or to their adopting children and bringing them up in an exclusive homosexual world. From all we know about children they need the influence of male and female figures in their life. That is not to say that parents do not abuse their children physically and sexually; some of them certainly do. But the perpetration of parental abuse is no justification for distorting the milieu in which children grow up.

Beyond the acceptance of homosexuals in the Christian community and the encouragement of stable personal relationships, Christians should try to ensure that homosexuals are not discriminated against in society. Part of the personal instability of male homosexuals is due to the social pressures they have to endure, so it is important that everyone in a position to help them achieve the realisation of their potential should do so.

In summary it can be said that homosexuals, like all minorities but particularly sexual minorities, threaten the heterosexual majority by their presence. Homosexuals are subject to major hostility and the Christian community shares in such prejudices. The overt condemnation of homosexuality by some churches, whatever its justification, heightens the problems faced by this community, which often feels persecuted.

Christianity nevertheless has an obligation to minister lovingly towards this group and it is essential to remember that Jesus Christ identified with minorities, not excluding sexual ones, who were persecuted. Christians feel ambivalent in this matter and are often caught in a trap, wanting to help the homosexual as a person but finding their practices difficult to accept. There is no need, of course, to accept the practices but there *is* an urgent need to rehabilitate homosexuals as persons if we are to save them from the scourge of AIDS.

27

Beyond AIDS there is always the nightmare for the Christian that, however clear the teaching on homosexuality appears to be, it might be open to essential modification, in which case we are placing false burdens on these men and women. The thought is haunting. So that in the matter of homosexuality, as in many other sexual issues, we have to watch and pray. On the one hand we must not lightly dismiss traditional teaching and on the other we must be conscious that in all matters – but particularly sexual ones – the need to see morality in a new light is a constant and urgent matter. It is imperative for the church to teach with authority; it is equally imperative to examine this teaching responsibly in the light of the ever evolving understanding of human nature and scriptural hermeneutics. Thus while agreeing that homosexuality undoubtedly diminishes the range of human possibilities inherent in heterosexuality, instead of emphasising its absolute objective 'disorder' status it may be more consistent with Christian thought to stress the elements of wounding to the personality and, in a much more appropriate psychological answer to the problem, the possibilities – however limited – of healing in personal relations of love, rather than condemning these efforts.

3

Sexual Behaviour in the West during the Last Twenty-Five Years

The campaign against AIDS is emphasising the nature of the disease, how it is transmitted and what precautions can be taken to prevent an epidemic. It is clear that AIDS is carried primarily through semen and blood and therefore one major form of prevention is abstinence from sexual activity in high risk situations. Such abstinence is lacking in the current campaign, set as it is against a background of marked sexual changes in the last twenty-five years. In this chapter evidence will be offered to substantiate the view that sexual behaviour has altered in ways which sharply contradict traditional Christian teaching.

During the last twenty-five years there has been a marked shift of emphasis from sexual discipline to permissiveness. Sex has been seen in terms of fun and pleasure, to be indulged in on the basis of natural physical and psychological needs. Increasingly the view has been taken that, as long as irresponsible procreation is avoided and the sexual act avoids coercion and pain, then it can be indulged in with impunity. This picture has been backed vigorously by the media and the ideas of control, discipline and consideration of the inner meaning of sex have not received serious hearing. Sexual education, in so far as it has gone, has emphasised this liberal attitude and been seriously concerned to instruct the young in effective methods of contraception. It is true to say that anyone who has not been persuaded by this sexual enthusiasm has been considered a deviant. Christianity has had a particularly hard time because its voice has been interpreted in terms

29

of warnings, prohibitions and the suppression of sexual joy. The climate of opinion seems to have been that one is either for unlimited sexual pleasure or against it. Positions have been polarised and on the one hand has stood liberated society, on the other Mrs Whitehouse and those who think like her. One of the aims of this book is to show that such violent opposition is unproductive. What is needed is for Christianity to accept unconditionally the goodness of sex and for society to realise that sex, like any other function, has purpose and meaning which demand control over its expression. This balanced view has not prevailed for the last twenty-five years. AIDS gives an opportunity to offer it to society for its serious consideration.

Contraception

The history of contraception extends from ancient times. Potions and local applications to the genitals have been widely used to prevent conception. Before the advent of the contraceptive pill in the early 1960s the commonest forms of contraception were barrier methods for women, withdrawal and condoms for men. The arrival of the contraceptive pill was a major revolution and its impact has been an enduring one ever since. In addition to the contraceptive pill, the intra-uterine device and sterilisation have added to the range of contraception. The acceptability of the contraceptive pill has varied as its safety has fluctuated in the light of successive reports but, despite some reservations, it has revolutionised contraception for women who no longer have to depend mainly on the man for safety against pregnancy.

As far as sexual behaviour is concerned the impact of a combination of liberated attitudes with safe contraception cannot be exaggerated. There is little doubt that women have been more easily persuaded to have intercourse than previously. Unfortunately this did not always mean that intercourse was accompanied by the use of contraception. Indeed part of the complexity of the sexual situation of the last two decades has been that the readiness to have sexual intercourse has not always been matched by preventive contraception.

The discrepancy undoubtedly contributed to pregnancies which were disposed of by abortion. To the Christian mind this has been a vicious circle of unmitigated evil.

There is little doubt that the availability of widespread contraception has not only increased sexual activity but, in the minds of many people, has separated the act of sexual intercourse from procreation. This has contributed to a fundamental transformation of sexual thinking. In the past intercourse had haunted women with the possibility of pregnancy. This fear has been greatly reduced and double sexual standards of the past have been replaced by a single pattern of behaviour. There are those who would maintain that the dissociation between coitus and procreation is so disastrous that every effort should be made to abolish the use of contraceptives, which, of course, is not going to happen.

The point that has to be made is that, although contraceptives have undoubtedly encouraged greater sexual activity, sexual behaviour is not going to be controlled ultimately by the absence or presence of contraceptives but by the fundamental social, psychological and moral attitudes to premarital and extramarital sexual behaviour. The absence of effective contraception in the past has not prevented periods of intense sexual activity outside marriage.

The only moral answer is to persuade mankind to use contraception in circumstances where it is appropriate, which really means defining when sexual intercourse should take place. As we shall see later, the Roman Catholic Church opposes the use of contraception even amongst the married. It is no secret that repeated surveys have shown that a majority of Roman Catholics have not been persuaded by the church in this matter. This suggests that, although there are many deficiencies in current contraceptives, their existence expresses a powerful and sophisticated advance by mankind in the practice of sexuality and I see no prospects whatsoever that such achievement will ever be given up, although vastly improved methods may emerge. What that means in practice is that sexual behaviour has to be regulated by an intelligent

31

understanding of its deepest meaning, which will be examined further in later chapters.

In the meantime there is overwhelming evidence that contraceptives are used widely by both married and single men and women. In one study 80 to 90 per cent of married women in their fertile years were using them and between 20 and 50 per cent of single women.

Premarital Intercourse

This increased use of contraception has coincided with a rise in premarital sexual activity. In the United States the Kinsey data have been reanalysed to cover the period 1938–63 showing that among teenagers some 40 per cent of white college males and 35 per cent of white college females had intercourse. Schofield's survey of British teenagers found comparable results in the early 1960s. Some ten years later another study showed a marked rise of teenage sexual activity, with an incidence of 69 per cent for boys and 55 per cent for girls. This increase has been documented also in the USA and in West Germany. In another study reported in Britain, single women were asked at different ages whether they had had sexual intercourse. The percentage rose from 11 per cent at age sixteen to 42 per cent by the age of twenty-three to twenty-four. In the same study the number of women who had sexual relations before marriage was to the order of 70 to 80 per cent. Furthermore some 95 per cent of single women who were in a sexual relationship in the mid-seventies used contraceptives. In the same study four-fifths of women in their early twenties approved of sexual intercourse. Thus there is no doubt that an increase in premarital sexual activity has occurred among western teenagers in the last twenty-five years.

But has this increased sexual activity been promiscuous, that is, frequent and with many different partners? As far as attitudes are concerned it is clear that sexual intercourse is not approved of indiscriminately. Very few women approve of premarital intercourse if it is promiscuous or if marriage is not to follow. With regard to frequency of premarital sexual intercourse, this is generally low – three-fifths of the sexually experienced had only ever had one partner – and half of those who had intercourse intended to marry their partner.

Thus the available evidence suggests there has been a widespread break with premarital virginity and thus with the strict Christian attitude, but the pattern of sexuality that emerges is not promiscuous. This conclusion is not always matched by the appearance given in the media. There the impression is often given that every night out is a sexual occasion. This is not the case; but the media may express views which are not representative of the country as a whole or, alternatively, offer an opportunity to write and talk about the world of sexual fantasy, which is always in sharp contrast to reality.

Abortion

I have suggested that a vicious circle exists in which increased sexual activity, not always safeguarded by adequate contraception, has led to increased abortion. Part of the orchestrated sexual clamour of the sixties was for a more liberal abortion policy. The grounds, pursued by the Abortion Law Reform Association, were a mixture of the appalling circumstances surrounding illegal abortion and the rights of women to have control over their own bodies. This view was widespread and led to considerable legislation throughout the West which liberated the law of abortion. In England and Wales 1967 was the year Parliament passed the Abortion Act. Effectively this Act allows termination of a pregnancy if two registered medical practitioners are of the opinion, formed in good faith, that the continuance of the pregnancy would involve greater risk to the life of the pregnant woman, or injury to her physical or mental health or that of any existing children of her family, than if it was allowed to continue. In fact the mental health clause allows any woman who wants an abortion to have it. Any woman who finds her pregnancy unacceptable or inconvenient can become depressed and her depression, with possible threat to her life, will allow any two doctors who are so minded to sign the necessary form and the abortion is carried out by gynaecologists who are sympathetic to terminations.

The ease with which abortions are carried out is shown by the figures for terminations. In 1969, soon after the Act came into operation, there were nearly 50,000 abortions in England and Wales. In 1985 there were 140,000. Of these, 87,000 were carried out on single women, 37,000 on married women and 16,000 on the widowed, divorced or separated.

There is little doubt that abortion, like other sexual matters, is open to much controversy. The discussion centres on the timetable of gestation within which the characteristics of a person are assumed. Some insist that life begins at the time of fertilisation. Others believe that some development must occur in the foetus before it can be said that a person exists. Both Aristotle and Thomas Aquinas accepted this view of delayed development, indeed Aquinas did not believe the foetus was ready to receive the human soul until forty days after fertilisation for males and eighty for females. These profound differences between male and female existed even for such a supremely rational person as Aquinas! Despite the view of Aquinas a number of eminent Christian theologians currently accept the view that personal human life begins some fourteen to twenty-one days after fertilisation. This interval is allowed to ensure that twinning or tripleting will no longer occur and so the organism's uniqueness is established. For practical purposes, direct abortion is not likely inside this timetable and the teaching of the Roman Catholic Church is that direct abortion is always wrong. It is a view with which I wholly concur and it is one in keeping with a morality based on person rather than biology. Biology treats the fertilised ovum as a mixture of genetic material with the potential of growth and development, whereas in fact a new person worthy of love develops after the implantation is completed and such a person is in a relationship of love with its mother and father: and so the life of the person is inviolate. This view of the sanctity of life has been present since ancient Greek times and, although constantly challenged, remains an essential part of Christian teaching. It is part of the Christian view of the sanctity of all life, life created in the image of God and therefore worthy of love.

There has been a steady opposition from all Christians to the Abortion Act 1967 ever since its inception, and particularly from the Roman Catholic community. Of course it is not enough to oppose laws: what is needed above all is to ensure prevention, and to alleviate distress in those women who find themselves in impossible personal situations.

Part of the answer to prevention is the exercise of sexual intercourse only in circumstances where a new life can be properly taken care of. With the best will in the world, however, women find themselves frequently in circumstances where new life will cause problems. It is imperative that the Christian community should not only legislate for the continuation of life, but also for the support of the mother.

While moral theologians continue to discuss and evaluate the morality of termination of pregnancy in extremely difficult circumstances, the fact is that the majority of abortions are carried out on healthy women with healthy babies and this is a continuation of serious injustice to the unborn person. Part of the moral revaluation of the future must be another look at the current abortion law. Meanwhile there is little doubt that the extensive incidence of abortion is part of the atmosphere of sexual permissiveness and it seems to me that the current figures of abortion should be a matter of great regret in the community.

Adultery

Continuing with the description of the changes in sexual behaviour in the last quarter of a century, we now move on to adultery. We know that there is a traditional Judaeo-Christian condemnation of adultery and we have the moving example in the Gospel of St John of our Lord's attitude towards the woman taken in adultery. The story is familiar but is worth repeating here:

35

The scribes and the Pharisees brought a woman along who had been caught committing adultery; and making her stand in the middle they said to Jesus, 'Master, this woman was caught in the very act of committing adultery, and in the Law Moses has ordered us to stone women of this kind. What have you got to say?' They asked him this as a test, looking for an accusation to use against him. But Jesus bent down and started writing on the ground with his finger. As they persisted with their question, he straightened up and said, 'Let the one among you who is guiltless be the first to throw a stone at her.' Then he bent down and continued writing on the ground. When they heard this they went away one by one, beginning with the eldest, until the last one had gone and Jesus was left alone with the woman, who remained in the middle. Jesus again straightened up and said, 'Woman, where are they? Has no one condemned you?' 'No one, sir,' she replied. 'Neither do I condemn you,' said Jesus. 'Go away, and from this moment sin no more.' (John 8:3–11)

This account is quoted in full as the paradigm of the Christian attitude to any violation of sexual morality. The task of Christianity is not to condemn but to love the person and, in the fullness of that love, the necessary change of attitude can occur. It is an example of how we should respond to all those infected with the HTLVIII/LAV virus and in particular to those who suffer from the disease of AIDS. While there is no end to the human possibilities and consequences of sexual violation of human integrity, the answer must always be forgiving love which rejoices in being in relationship with the person concerned.

Unlike the permissiveness shown in our time towards premarital sexual intercourse, a much stricter attitude has been preserved towards adultery. All recent surveys show that fidelity remains a high value. As far as figures are concerned the Kinsey data of over forty years ago showed that some 34 per cent of married men and 20 per cent of married women admitted to adultery. Recent American work shows no increase in extramarital activity from the Kinsey figures. Other studies show some increase in male adultery.

The persistent and widespread condemnation of adultery arises from the fact that society as a whole can see the violation of personal love involved in this act. Spouses owe loyalty to one another. Extramarital intercourse involves a rejection of the partner, who feels hurt and dismissed. Adultery goes against the very nature of commitment and bonding and, in so far as both of these are experiences deeply embedded in human nature, their contradiction arouses deep feelings of anxiety, anger and distress.

Adultery is directly relevant to AIDS. As we have seen, homosexuality involves a wide spectrum of sexual expression from the exclusively homosexual to the bisexual person. It is also well documented that some husbands with bisexual tendencies may have intercourse with a homosexual partner, become infected and then transmit the virus to their wives. We meet these situations in the course of marital work in which either spouse, but particularly the husband, has an extramarital affair which is homosexual. In addition to the trauma of discovering that their husband or wife has these leanings, in future spouses will also have to counter the anxiety of becoming infected with the AIDS virus.

Although adultery carried out in the context of homosexuality is likely to be rare, intercourse with a female prostitute will not be uncommon. Here it is important to remind the reader that so far infection of AIDS from women to men is rare, given that the virus is carried in semen and in blood. Nevertheless the reality is that more prostitutes will become infected and a pool of the virus will exist in the vagina and cervical fluids of women. It may be that women will not become an important source of virus dissemination but caution should be exercised until we know a great deal more about the routes of infection.

Thus while adultery certainly plays a part in the total sexual picture of the period under consideration, it can be said with some confidence that faithfulness is still important to people. Although adultery may play a part in AIDS epidemiology it is not likely to be a major contribution to the spread of the disease.

Marital Breakdown

Just as there was a major impetus for change in the law on abortion, so a similar drive occurred for changes in the law on divorce. Extensive discussion in the sixties culminated in the Divorce Reform Act 1969. In this Act 'irretrievable breakdown of marriage' became the sole ground for petitioning for divorce. The Act lays down:

> The Court hearing a petition for divorce shall not hold the marriage to have broken down irretrievably unless the petitioner satisfies the court of one or more of the following facts, that is to say:–
>
> (a) that the respondent has committed adultery and the petitioner finds it intolerable to live with the respondent;
>
> (b) that the respondent has behaved in such a way that the petitioner cannot reasonably be expected to live with the respondent;
>
> (c) that the respondent has deserted the petitioner for a continuous period of at least two years immediately preceding the presentation of the petition;
>
> (d) that the parties to the marriage have lived apart for a continuous period of at least two years immediately preceding the presentation of the petition and the respondent consents to a decree being granted;
>
> (e) that the parties to the marriage have lived apart for a continuous period of at least five years immediately preceding the presentation of the petition.

Until 1984 no petition could be presented to a court in the first three years of marriage except in exceptional circumstances. The Family Proceedings Act 1984 removed this prohibition and a petition can now be presented after one year of marriage.

There is little doubt in my mind that these legal changes in Britain mean effectively that the law offers no protection whatsoever to the stability of marriage. In this ultimate situation what support can be offered must come from the community and the religious bodies.

As the situation stands the number of divorces in England and Wales is now around the 160,000 mark (figures for 1985) and compared with 25,000 in 1961 show over a sixfold increase in the period under consideration. Every year some half a million men, women and children leave the divorce courts. One in five children under the age of sixteen will find themselves in a broken home and at current rates one in three marriages are heading for dissolution.

Given the central role of the family in society and in Christian thought, I have stated that this massive increase in marital breakdown is the single most serious social evil of western society (although I want to make it absolutely clear that in no sense are the couple themselves involved in divorce evil). The consequences are massive, the personal agonies of the couple involved often acute and my greatest regret has been, and continues to be, that the Roman Catholic Church has been more concerned with other sexual matters such as contraception and abortion than with marital breakdown. While I am in total sympathy with the concern over abortion, I take the view that marital breakdown eclipses that evil. For me divorce stands out as the prime example of the devastation of personal love.

In terms of AIDS marital breakdown is relevant in that alienated spouses are very likely to seek comfort sexually with more than one other partner and, since the disease may be transmitted heterosexually, there is a grave danger that the particular vulnerability of the divorced person could add to the pool of potential sexual promiscuity.

Sexual Minorities

In addition to the major sexual changes recorded above, the epoch under consideration has seen the outspokenness of

39

sexual minorities, in particular homosexuality and the sexual needs of those who are normally called deviants with a predilection for fetishism, transvestism, transsexualism, sadomasochism – a world hitherto confined to fringe literature – and finally the sexual needs of the handicapped. All these themes have surfaced in books and the media and an attempt has been made to introduce them into sexual education. While society has certainly been open to becoming informed, we cannot say that much advance has been made in basic understanding, sympathy and compassion in these areas, with the possible exception of homosexuality where homosexuals over the age of twenty-one can indulge in sexual activity legally in private.

Assessment of the Last Quarter of a Century

To conclude this chapter I want to emphasise that the last quarter of a century has been a period of intense social, psychological and moral activity in the field of personal relationships involving sexual activity and its consequences. On the whole it has seen a heightened sexual involvement in which an attempt has been made to sweep away fear, prohibitions and taboos. Thus it is very difficult to persuade a teenager today that premarital intercourse should be avoided. It is certainly scarcely possible to persuade men and women of all ages to avoid the use of contraceptives on rational grounds. That is not to say that reason predominates and young people always use them; that is far from the case. But contraceptive-free intercourse is considered to be a human frailty. In fact it is hard to find anyone who would condemn contraceptives except a tiny minority of Roman Catholics.

Beyond premarital coitus there is the easy availability of abortion, if and when the unwanted pregnancy arrives. Despite this ease of procuring an abortion the evidence suggests that termination of pregnancy carries some guilt and other emotional reactions and a number of women have reservations about its rightfulness. It is only in extreme feminist circles that the advocacy of a totally permissive atti-tude to abortion exists. But even with these reservations the fact is that thousands of women do resort to it and the avail-able surveys suggest that in the immediate aftermath women who have had terminations are not overwhelmed with guilt, although there are always exceptions.

Within marriage itself adultery continues to occur as it has always done, but there has not been a marked increase either in incidence or of approval. It still remains a disapproved activity, even if much greater tolerance is shown towards it.

As far as the stability of marriage is concerned there have been marked changes towards instability and western society has seen a wave of divorce which, at its highest, may involve one in two marriages.

Finally, against these individual changes, there has been a rise of interest in the life of sexual minorities and the sexuality of the handicapped. In both these areas sexual activity is no longer a taboo.

From the point of view of the discipline required by AIDS against indiscriminate sexual activity, clearly the climate of opinion in sexual matters could not facilitate sexual absti-nence. In fact the present campaign against AIDS has hardly made an attempt to encourage an attitude of sexual restraint and control. The absence of such a view reflects what has transpired in the last quarter of a century. While it cannot be said that during this period the scene has been set for promiscuity, it has certainly facilitated sexual activity.

From the Christian point of view the general trend has been most disquieting although, as we shall see in Chapter 4, the situation is complex. What I am describing here is the negative side but there is also a positive side which has to be taken into account as well.

4

Evaluation of Sexuality in the Last Twenty-Five Years

We have examined the negative side of the sexual revolution, described in Chapter 3. The result has been to mobilise a number of forces in society which see the past quarter of a century as an unmitigated disaster. But that is not the case. Much has been achieved during this period and the record has to be set straight by describing the gains.

The changes of the last twenty-five years have to be seen against a background in which sexuality was often considered a guilty secret. The subject was rarely mentioned at home or at school or in society at large, and when it was touched upon it was surrounded by an embarrassing awkwardness. As a doctor I have to take the histories of patients every day and as a lecturer I have been privileged to listen to the accounts of many people in this country and abroad. Those who grew up before or just after the war were often treated to a combination of silence, prohibitions and taboos. In Roman Catholic schools there was an excessive preoccupation with chastity and little concern for the wonder and beauty of human sexuality. Instead of proclaiming this precious gift of God, young boys and girls were either kept ignorant or conditioned to guilt in such matters as nakedness, sexual attraction and masturbation. The introduction to sin for many boys was the subject of masturbation.

Those generations have not forgiven Christianity for its negative attitude, nor is there any evidence that Christianity would have attempted to correct its ways if it had not been pushed by a secular world that rebelled against such restrictions. It is easy to criticise Roman Catholicism for its strictures and the presence of celibate priests and nuns in its schools, but the inhibitions were widespread and prevailed well outside the Roman Catholic boundaries. Above all, such fears were not only having a devastating effect on the sexual lives of the participants but were undoubtedly a contributing factor in the mass withdrawal from church life witnessed over the period we are considering.

I am a product of that generation and have tried to do all I can to restore to Christian thought a proper appreciation of one of the Creator's greatest donations to mankind. Indeed I have marvelled at the history of Christianity which has been so indifferent to the basis of the man-woman union and the formation of the family. Without sexual attraction the world would not be recognisable in its present form and the lack of positive attention paid by Christianity to sexuality is one of its greatest deficiencies, particularly as the scriptures are laden with positive references to it. There is no lack of indication suggesting that the Creator wants us to celebrate this gift.

Perhaps the greatest achievement of recent times is the move by western society to celebrate sexuality. Those who fear sexuality will attack the changes as nothing more than a return to unbridled instinct. There is always the hostility of those who cannot cope with sexuality in their own lives. Sex can be reduced to instinct, trivialised; and undoubtedly there exists an exploitive element in every society that moves in the direction of the sale of pornography – sexual titillation – for the separation between sex and love are constant distortions and they will always be fostered. But this should never be made an excuse for undervaluing or suppressing the importance of this unique gift of God.

The overwhelming efforts of the last twenty-five years have been to rehabilitate sex in its richness and preciousness and a great deal has been achieved in that direction.

To start with, the subject is no longer taboo. It is possible to talk, write and broadcast about it widely and there has been a revolution against secrecy, which is a permanent achievement and must never again be lost. The last twenty-five years should not be seen as just another historical epoch of sexual liberty. Historians will point out previous such periods which have been replaced by overall oppression and pessimism. I would like to think that the recent efforts will endure. These efforts have spread in the schools and sexual education is now accepted as part of the curriculum. It is possible to criticise these educational efforts. They often contain too much biology and too little emphasis on the loving aspects of personal relations, which calls for urgent correction.

Beyond the school, society has made considerable efforts to advance the knowledge of men and women with regard to their sexual lives. The advent of sexual therapy initiated by the work of Masters and Johnson in America has revolutionised our thinking in the practical aspects of helping people with their sexual problems. Magazines and books have abounded with sexual instruction. We have a long way to go yet but a good start has been made.

Working with married couples all over western society we have come to recognise how important sex is for maintaining human bonds. In particular women are calling for a more affectionate response on the part of men and education has much to achieve in helping boys to realise that sex is much more than a physical adventure.

Indeed what we are discovering as a society is the need to go beyond words. The battle to make sex better publicised has been won and this is a great achievement of the recent decades. What has yet to be realised is the promulgation of an awareness of sex which is combined with affection and love. This should be one of the specific tasks that emerge from rethinking sexual matters as a result of the AIDS situation. Christianity must emerge as a champion of loving sex. It has to accept unconditionally the goodness of sex, yet insist that its proper place is only in the context of a loving relationship.

In the course of the sexual revolution that has achieved so much good, there have also emerged men and women who wish to separate sex from love. I have read their views and met them in debates. For them sex is its own justification and needs no connection with love. This view is as wrong as was

44

the neglect of the past. It is for this reason that I want Christianity to accept unequivocally the advances made on behalf of sexuality and from now on become the champion of an integrated approach in which the essential human characteristic of love is conjoined to sexuality. Such an approach is the hallmark of this book and is the answer not only to sexual behaviour but ultimately to the control of AIDS.

AIDS offers a historic situation for Christianity to reassess its position and become the champion of loving sex. This position is long overdue and now is an appropriate opportunity for reassessment. This means that Christianity must invite its people and the experts to describe sexual love and, while keeping a vigilant eye against distortion, to proclaim it with all its might around the world.

The second major event in this recent history is that, in addition to proclaiming the goodness of sex, society has moved significantly from seeing the basis of sexuality as biological to being personal. This shift has not yet been examined in detail but it is unequivocally there.

The single most important contribution has been the advent of widespread birth regulation. I use the words birth regulation because I want to stress the profound significance of the change in human attitudes and thought whereby the size of the family has been considerably reduced, independently of the means taken to achieve it. Within the Roman Catholic world the issue is still the morality of contraception. But the real point is well beyond this discussion. In western society a combination of material welfare, medical advances whereby the overwhelming majority of commenced pregnancies continue successfully to the end with the baby surviving afterwards, and the arrival of sophisticated psychology, have persuaded parents not only to have smaller families but to nurture those children to an infinitely higher degree in wholeness and integrity. It is always dangerous to predict, but if the rest of the world advances in this direction then the size of the family will be reduced throughout the globe and the emphasis will be on the appropriate social, cognitive, emotional and spiritual education.

In other words the whole world has to take aboard the fact that having achieved the desired family size, 99 per cent of sexual activity within marriage will be consciously and deliberately non-procreative. Hitherto society and Christianity have based their thinking on a biological, procreative basis for sexuality. From now on we have to recognise that the main purpose of sexuality is a personal encounter whose main basis must be love. Christianity has not seriously begun to examine the implications of this shift and until it does it cannot come to terms with contemporary sexuality. The Roman Catholic Church is making a last-ditch battle to avoid the implications of this transformation through its stand over contraception but its own people have moved on by accepting contraception. Everyone has to see that we are in the midst of a large-scale revolution and we need to discuss the implications.

How large the change is can be seen from the basis of sexual morality in the past. A great deal of our sexual ethics has been based on biology. The medieval theologians believed that procreation was the natural goal, purpose or finality of sexuality because it is this finality which human beings share with the animal kingdom. Thus the biological, procreative dimension became the basis for sexual morality, and that means that for sexual intercourse to be moral there must be the deposit of semen in the vagina.

As a result of this understanding of the natural law, sexual sins fall into two categories. There are sins against nature where semen is not deposited in the vagina, such as masturbation, anal intercourse, oral intercourse, orgasm attained by the caressing of the female genitalia, contraception and, in rare cases, intercourse with animals. There are also sins where the biological aspects are respected but the human ones violated, such as fornication, adultery, rape and incest. But, even in these situations, procreation is in mind in traditional theology, for in all these cases intercourse is possible but the offspring would not have a pair of parents to nurture it. This creativity with its biological overtones has played a crucial component in sexual morality.

The link between sexual intercourse and procreation is so intimately intertwined and has formed the foundation of moral thought for so long that I receive letters showing astonishment at my very temerity in questioning it, ignoring the fact that western society has moved on beyond this point of thought. If morality does not take heed of the change there will be no one left to hear the message of yesterday.

In fairness it has to be said that some Roman Catholic theologians have grasped this point but the Roman Catholic Church as a whole has not and the conflict over contraception is a symptom of a profound difference of evaluating human sexuality.

Basing the moral law on the equivalence of animal and human behaviour through the common link of biology is fundamentally wrong, in that human beings are always far more than animals and have to be assessed as such: but apart from this, the fact is that sexuality between men and women is a personal encounter which has to be judged only by authentic human attributes. The assessment of sexuality on the basis of depositing sperm in the vagina is a crude and totally unsatisfactory criterion of evaluation. It is not therefore surprising that Christianity is in such a turmoil as to how to advise young people in contemporary society.

The shift away from procreation means that there is now a choice in the pursuit of sexual intercourse between seeing it purely as a source of fun and pleasure and making pleasure serve human love. Everyone concerned about an authentic human sexuality is worried that the shift from procreation, particularly with the large-scale emergence of contraception, will lead to the alternative, the pleasure of the orgasm. This is a choice which exchanges one form of biology for another. Instead of basing morality on the deposition of semen in the vagina, we now count orgasms. Such a hedonistic approach leaves out a considerable dimension of human attributes in the sexual encounter and the seeking of pleasure is as limited a goal as the biology approach from which we are just emerging.

In conclusion it can be said that the last quarter of a century has seen the dual advantages of freeing sexuality from the claims of furtive silence and from a morality based upon biology which has prevailed for many centuries. These are substantial gains and demand a fundamental new approach to the subject.

5

Reassessment of Sexuality

The point has been made that there have been pronounced changes in recent times in evaluating sexuality. A combination of the goodness of sex and a pronounced move away from the biology of procreation has emerged. But what has also risen is a hedonism in which sexual pleasure has become a dominant theme. In terms of ethics we are faced with a traditional morality which made procreation the paramount value from which sexuality drew its meaning, and a crude pleasure-seeking policy which has made the campaign against AIDS synonymous with the condom. Is there an alternative which can do justice to traditional human and scriptural thought? In this chapter an outline for an alternative ethical basis is given in which love and personal relationships are offered as the ultimate ground for sexual morality. Personal relationships are the stuff from which human beings derive their greatest meaning, and within these encounters the majority of men and women long for affection and love. Christianity's most profound belief is that God is love, lives in a mystery of relationship in his own life, and has created the world and mankind to share in his life. I find it very difficult to understand how the Roman Catholic Church can persist with a morality based largely on the biology of procreation when the alternative is clearly so much more in tune with the revelation that we have from God himself about love.

A sexual morality based on a theology of loving relationship also reflects the psychology of the past half-century, which is infinitely preferable to the outmoded biology of the Middle Ages. It is vital to consider this psychology, for its components reflect the 'higher' elements of human beings, raising them well above the instinctual level of animal activity. What one wants to do is to rescue Christianity from a situation where it offers love as the ultimate meaning of human behaviour but still shapes its understanding of sexual conduct on the similarity between human and animal behaviour; for it is this contradiction that reduces the persuasiveness of its teaching.

That is not to say that instincts do not play a part in the human personality. They certainly do and it is well known that Freud conceived his theory of the human personality as being based on the dual instincts of sexuality and aggression. But generations of his successors have modified this position and it is very damaging to the Christian cause when the accumulated psychological knowledge still lies at the periphery of its thinking.

Psychology is therefore at the centre of our thought and a brief review is given of how the child grows, and the role of sexuality and love play in this development.

A baby's sex is primarily determined by the presence of the X and Y chromosomes, with a girl having an XX and the boy an XY configuration. These chromosomes determine the external genitalia; thereafter boys and girls are brought up according to the cultural expectations of particular societies. There is endless and unresolved discussion of how much of the male and female characteristics are contributed to by genetic influence, the result of what is called nature, and the part that is played by upbringing or nurture. Thus little boys and girls are dressed differently, given different toys, are encouraged to play different games and are generally treated in different ways. This separation continues throughout life and is responsible for those differences which form the complementarity of the sexes and leads to a theology of complementary self-giving. The experiences of the child in the hands of its parents, relatives, teachers and friends are part of its social learning and growth but the content will vary from country to country, reflecting the social mores of each area. In addition to its social upbringing the child has the possibility of developing its cognitive potential. Educational psychology

50

owes a great deal to Piaget whose research is the guiding light for the educational development of children throughout the world. Finally there is the dynamic development of the child which accounts for the growth of its affective life, the world of feelings and emotions. It is the affective life that is most closely linked with what we call love; a close affinity between Christianity and this psychological dimension is one of the still-awaited basic advances in Christian thinking. One of the reasons for this delay is that some of the greatest contributors to dynamic psychology have lived and worked in Britain and the United States. Despite the presence of Freud and Jung in Europe, the critical later developments of such people as Klein, Winnicott and Bowlby in Britain and Fromm, Horney, Sullivan and Erickson in the United States have not penetrated the inner world of Christianity, and yet if we are to understand sexuality we must fully understand their work.

Formation of Attachment

The most important figure in the field of sexuality is John Bowlby, not for his specific contribution to sexuality as such but for his concepts of human attachment. Bowlby states (I paraphrase) that until the mid-1950s human bonds were conceived on the basis of the reduction of certain drives, food in infancy and sex in adulthood, and for this to happen another human being is necessary. Bowlby has shown in his work that this view of bonding does not do justice to human behaviour. Instead he shows that from the first few weeks of life, and continuously thereafter, human beings have the capacity to form attachments. Attachment behaviour is conceived as any form of behaviour that results in a person attaining or retaining proximity to some other differentiated and preferred individual, who is usually conceived as stronger, wiser or more attractive. Attachment behaviour characterises human beings from cradle to grave. The importance of Bowlby's theory is that the 'other' assumes a much greater significance than as a mere source of instinctual relief. Such a view plays a prominent part in Christian thought where one of the principal reasons opposing fornication and adultery is the use of another person as a sexual object.

What Bowlby proposes is that the infant, from the first few weeks of life, is able to make an attachment to the mother which has affectional connections. The attachment is formed primarily through touch, vision and sound. The young infant stabilises the relationship by familiarising itself with the mother's face and gradually the rest of her body: this is the recognition of vision. Concurrently the young child becomes acquainted with the sound of her voice: this is the recognition of sound. Finally an intimate connection is formed with touch through holding and being held. This triad of sensory stimuli allows the baby to become bonded to the mother so that she becomes essential for life. The baby not only gets attached to the mother but also to the father and other key persons who form a continuous presence in his life.

This 'attachment', which has some link with Lorenz's work on imprinting, was a major advance on Freudian thought which saw mother's role principally in terms of food provider. Attachment theory has important repercussions for the development of affection and love, for it is within the bond of affection formed between mother and child, and later father and child, that the essential human interaction of growth and development will take place. It means that significant interaction, which is worthy of the name 'human', always occurs in the context where affective feelings are present. This differentiates the personal dimension of human relationships from the impersonal, where roles are exchanged such as are necessary for work and the transaction of social life. Since sex is such a fundamentally human experience it loses its vitality when it occurs in the absence of an affectionate personal interaction.

Forming an attachment such as the one that is transacted between mother and child is the first experience of 'falling in love'. The growing person falls in love first with several key people in its life who will successively become his friends, and finally with one person, his spouse. When we think of what is entailed in 'falling in love' we see how much vision, sound and touch play their parts. We fall in love with people whose appearance and characteristics we like, whose voice we find pleasing and with whom we feel comfortable in physical proximity. In the course of my work with married couples I come across the phenomenon of falling 'out of love'. Here the process is the reverse when we are no longer excited by the appearance of our spouse, whose looks no longer stir us, whose voice is no longer pleasant and comforting and whose body no longer promotes a longing of affection or sexual desire.

People fall 'in' and 'out' of love in friendships and marriage. One of the challenges for Christianity which lays so much stress on both is to find the psychological reasons for the loss of attachment. But if the attachment is still present, any breaking of the bond leads to anxiety, anger and depression. The young baby offers adults a prototype of the reaction to the temporary absence of mother. The baby in the cot wakes up and, if it can, stands up and look round the room to find the mother. This is the scanning we all do in the process of searching for someone we love. If the baby does not find the mother or is not reassured by the sound of her voice it becomes alarmed and begins to cry. In the adult also continuous absence raises an alarm reaction; this can be felt as anxiety, which is experienced as a sensation in the 'pit of the stomach', palpitations, sweating and dry mouth. We do not have these feelings for people who are not significant in our life and with whom we have no affectionate bonds. When the mother does not appear, or when she has gone away, is in hospital or has died, the baby continues to cry but now in anger and deep distress. The adult also turns to tears when the beloved has gone. Finally continuous absence brings sadness and misery and is what the young child experiences at the loss of its mother. The adult grieves the loss of a dear friend or spouse in a similar way.

Attachment theory is fundamental to our understanding of sexual behaviour. It is vital to assert with strong conviction that sexual intercourse is such a fundamental expression of unity between persons that human authenticity requires the presence of an affective attachment to do full justice to its meaning.

Within the context of this attachment, which is the framework for human growth, several key experiences begin to develop in each successive year of life. The point I want to stress here is that in the course of our development most of us are conditioned to experience our significant moments within a context of affection. This link between significant wants and affection is crucial to coitus, and the hallmark of chastity is the conjunction of sexual activity and affection. The separation of the two is one of the features of dehumanisation.

Unity between Instinct and Person

Looking at the first year of life we find three psychologists who have made vital contributions here: D. W. Winnicott, E. H. Erickson and M. Klein. Of these neo-Freudians the first two are more pertinent to the line of thought followed here.

According to Winnicott the baby develops a psyche in the first year of life which is to be distinguished from the mind. The psyche becomes an increasingly organised inner world of the child in which its somatic experiences are paramount. What the baby experiences physically becomes part of its psyche and already in this first year of life a distinction is made between what feels 'good' and what feels 'bad'. That which is good is acceptable to the emerging ego and that which is bad is unacceptable, feels persecutory and is rejected. What Winnicott brings out is the intimate link between physical instinctual experiences and feeling good. At this stage of life the instinctual is largely based on food and elimination. The ingestion and elimination of food has an orgastic quality. Hunger is associated with excitement and a state of readiness, ingestion with satisfaction and relief; and in all children elimination has a quality of explosive relief after the build up of tension. The infant is thus learning the sequence of desire, physical want and satisfaction: the sexual sequence of adult coitus has been prepared for and anticipated by the ingestion of food, which is decisively felt as something good. But gradually the child learns control from within, that is, having to wait for food and postponing satisfaction. For Winnicott this is the beginning of morality based on inner control: pursuing this line of thought, a later morality based on control of sexual feelings will not be foreign to the person's inner world. Winnicott makes the significant point that, while it is possible to acquire this self-control over instincts, it is nevertheless difficult. The child has the task of controlling the ruthless demands of internal instinct, which is no easy one. But in this respect it *is* helped by a loving mother whose strictures, made in love, save the child from having to fight alone the fierceness of self-control. What Winnicott is trying to show is that control over instincts, waiting for food – indeed wanting and doing without a whole range of pleasures – is something that the child learns more easily when boundaries are laid down by a loving parent who, the child learns, loves and cares for it. For Winnicott this natural evolution of self-control, in the presence of a favourable parental environment, brings about self-discipline without the loss of spontaneity.

In terms of sexuality Winnicott's views are paramount to the upbringing of the child. The child has to learn self-control – which in fact often means being unselfish, having to suppress its personal wishes for the sake of others – and yet must retain a feeling that its impulses are good.

It is well established that in the early years of life the little boy may experience sexual erections or play with his penis and the little girl with her genitals. How these experiences are handled by the parents is of the greatest importance. On the one hand there can be harsh, negative prohibitions associating disgust and fear with these childish sexual activities, and on the other reassurance, approbation and a distinct feeling given that the genitalia are part of the whole body, which is good. In this way the child associates good feelings with the antecedents of its adult sexual life.

Essential to Winnicott's thinking is that the sense of love develops from the very beginning of life. Thus for the child the meaning of 'love' alters as it grows. Love first means existing, breathing and being alive. Love then means appetite,

55

no awareness of the other person but simply need and satisfaction. Then love comes to mean affectionate concern for mother; and finally love means an integration on the part of the child of mother as a source of instinctual experience and of affectionate contact: so later taking and giving will be interrelated. As far as the main theme of this book is concerned (the integrated experience of coitus with affection) the root of this integration is laid down in childhood; indeed from the very first year of life.

The genius of Winnicott is to show that the human psyche is the product of the earliest experiences of the physical in relation to the affectionate, and that the earliest physical dimension is instinctual. Thus the psyche learns self-control as the direct result of a combination of personal control and parental facilitation, a facilitation which is gradually internalised and makes the young adult a person who can, in the context of affection, control his instincts. I emphasise Winnicott as a psychologist who shows clearly, as many dynamic psychologists do, the essential human integration of instincts with the growing person, an integration which feels and is good, has its ultimate meaning in the context of a loving relationship and is open to control. Many sophisticated critics of traditional sexual morality argue that there is no essential connection between coitus, that is, instinct, and personal love. But in terms of depth psychology, such a link is present if one traces the growth of the child in its dynamic aspects. Here instinct is part of the goodness of life which grows within the context of the loving parent-child relationship.

Returning to the first year of life, Erickson has developed an outline of human dynamic development based on key human experiences. In this first year, he states, a basic sense of trust is established. This is created by the mother combining a sensitive care of the baby's individual needs and a firm personal trustworthiness within the trusted framework of the cultural lifestyle.

In the context of human relationships the sense of trust is supreme. It is the criterion by which we feel safe in personal relationships and this trust extends to social, physical and emotional parameters of the interaction. We trust the person we recognise as similar to us in their social characteristics. We trust someone with whom we feel physically safe. We trust someone with whom we feel in tune emotionally. As far as sexual intercourse is concerned there is a natural desire to have intercourse with someone we trust, who is like us, makes us feel safe and gives us the impression of wanting and caring for us. At one end of the scale is intercourse in the context of trusting love and at the other is to be found the experience of rape.

Erickson then moves on to the second and third year of life where he describes the acquisition of a sense of autonomy and how it relates to its opposites – shame and doubt. The second and third years of life are supremely suited to this concept of autonomy, being the years when the child learns to crawl, stand, walk, talk, dress and feed itself. In the acquisition of these characteristics the child and the mother interact powerfully. The child learns by trial and error; its primary efforts are either appreciated and praised or treated in a derisory way and criticised. Either the mother praises its efforts or is unwilling to be patient and takes over from the child, making it feel hopeless and helpless. For Erickson the autonomy stage becomes decisive for the ratio of love and hate, co-operation and wilfulness, freedom of self-expression and its suppression. From a sense of self-control without loss of self-esteem comes a lasting sense of goodwill and pride; from a sense of loss of self-control and intrusive over-control comes a lasting propensity towards doubt and shame.

There are other crucial events that occur in the second and third years of life. In the process of acquiring the various skills the child wants to do things in its own way and the mother in hers. Inevitably, as can be seen in any household where there are toddlers, there is a clash and the frustrated mother gets angry, shouts and even smacks. This is a momentous moment. For the first time the child experiences external anger and aggression. It feels its actions are bad and it feels bad and guilty. It is temporarily cut off from the love of

57

mother. It is a moment of devastation. But soon it is over. The mother forgives, the child feels sorry and reconciliation is soon at hand. But the cycle of anger, conflict, guilt, reparation and reconciliation endures throughout life and is an essential part of love.

Furthermore when the child experiences this conflict it feels temporarily bad and mother is also experienced as momentarily bad. Thus both mother and himself can be felt as good and bad. The ability to experience both ourselves and others as bad and good at the same time is part of what we call ambivalence, that is, having contradictory feelings towards persons. At the heart of love is our ability to feel more positive than negative about ourselves, and to treat others with more love than anger or hate.

In the fourth and fifth year of life Erickson believes the child acquires the sense of initiative. The child now plans undertakings and 'attacks' tasks with the desire to be active and on the move. By now the child also develops two other characteristics. By the end of the third year a toddler can spend some time away from its mother at the infant school. This is known as a process of 'internalisation'. The child can internalise mother, keep her alive in imagination and have a sense of her in her physical absence. In this way it can spend a few hours away from her feeling safe and secure. The ability to internalise significant persons in our life is crucial to human relationships. It is this ability which keeps alive in us the presence of another person when they are absent and is a vital characteristic for fidelity when we are away for periods from those we love. People who cannot internalise will quickly feel alone and desolate. This is called loneliness and the resort to other women and men by spouses who are separated from their wives and husbands depends a great deal on the psychological capacity to internalise their partner. In addition to internalisation the child at this age becomes much more conscious of the feelings of being recognised, wanted and appreciated and has a much clearer idea of the difference between acceptance and rejection.

58

School

There follow the school years, when the child leaves the world of intimate relationship of one-to-one encounters with its parents and enters the world of many children in the community of the school. Here it learns a number of skills which Erickson describes with the term 'industry'. He learns to earn recognition by producing things. The child receives systematic instruction in order to accomplish things which gradually supersede the whims of play. There is no question about the importance of being proficient in the three Rs. But the great danger in school life is the attitude of parents who make approval conditional on scholastic achievement. In this situation the child gets the feeling that its lovability depends on the success of work rather than on its own intrinsic goodness. This is an attitude that can mar its whole life as it continues, beyond school, to attach greater importance to work and achievement than to love and personal relationships.

There are other features of school life which are important for the child. It now has to live in an impersonal world where rules and regulations govern behaviour. In this way it is introduced to another sense of love which is to be found in the concept of social justice. The school is the first society outside the home where love is to be understood not in terms of personal exchanges but rather for the good of others, who may be poor, different in colour, social class or economic standing, or deprived. The school begins to mirror the wider society which the grown up will enter, where is to be found the rule of law, impersonality and competition, and also the need for social justice.

The reader may wonder why I have pursued the development of the child beyond the first year when he forms an attachment or learns to fall in love with a significant 'other' person. The reason is that beyond this initial experience the growing child learns the meaning of love in the context of its *development* and the interaction with its parents, teachers and relatives. So much of the sexual atmosphere portrayed in our media and in the AIDS campaign is restricted to the *moment* of falling in love, which is equated with having sexual intercourse. But in the course of real life there are two significant sequences in personal relationships. First one falls in love with another man or woman, and then one proceeds to love that person. The world of reality is not some fantasy about a constant state of being in love, but rather about how to maintain the critical relationship of loving for over fifty years. In the context of loving we not only have to recognise, accept and respect the beloved but we have to have a real understanding of their autonomy and initiative. We have to maintain trust, communicate, resolve conflicts, forgive, and preserve a balance between intimacy and separateness; in other words put into operation all the experiences we have acquired in the course of our upbringing.

As mentioned earlier in this chapter there are two intimate experiences of love in life. So much of the distortion of the world of love in contemporary society is the wide assumption that the word only applies to the process of falling in love, which is equated with going to bed. Crucial as coitus is, most couples retain their loving relationships outside bed; what happens *in* bed is heavily conditioned by the quality of the relationship *outside* it. But in the campaign against AIDS it is instant love-making that is highlighted, which is a distortion of real life.

Puberty and Adolescence

Somewhere between the ages of ten and fourteen puberty arrives with the development of the secondary sexual characteristics. The boy's genitalia reach adult size, the voice breaks and the body is covered with adult hair distribution. In particular the young man begins to shave and the testicles produce semen. The girl begins her monthly periods, her breasts develop and her hair takes its distinctive pubic distribution. Her external genitalia develop and internally her uterus enlarges, while her ovaries begin to ovulate. Sexual penetration can now occur and so, soon, can pregnancy.

All these physical changes are accomplished by marked psychological ones. The adolescent distances himself or herself sexually from the parents, particularly the parent of the opposite sex. This sexual withdrawal is accompanied by heterosexual attraction and the increasing interest of the two sexes in each other develops.

With this growing mutual interest fantasies abound and the walls of boys' bedrooms are plastered with feminine figures while those of girls are similarly covered with the heroes of the moment. There is a growing and intense awareness of each other.

Adolescence is said to last from about the age of twelve to the early twenties. It is a period where, as we have seen, there has been marked increased sexual activity. The present campaign against AIDS has assumed its continuity and is strongly advising the use of condoms. My concern here is not with the use of condoms as contraceptives but the philosophy which advocates coitus during adolescence.

Adolescence is a period when young people have to assert their independence, start work or advanced study and, with particular reference to their sexuality, become familiar with themselves as sexual persons and discover the world of heterosexuality. Erickson calls this phase one of identity and role confusion, by which he means that the young person is on the top step of childhood and the bottom one of adulthood. One moment he feels grown up and the next, at times of crisis, difficulty or illness, he regresses to the dependence of childhood. If further studies are undertaken financial dependence on parents may continue. Living under the same roof as the parents brings the conflicts between the desire for autonomy by the young person and the conformity demanded by parents who feel it very difficult to accept their child as a grown up man or woman. Most households in western society go through the chaos of reconciling these differences and the overwhelming majority of them emerge successfully.

In the field of sexuality this is a period of discovery, not primarily or necessarily of genital activity. The first discovery of one's sexuality is often to be found in masturbation. For a previous generation masturbation was often associated with acute anxiety and moral guilt. Many young boys first discovered the meaning of sin after puberty in the confession that they had masturbated. Within the framework of a biological basis to sexual morality, masturbation is intrinsically evil within the Roman Catholic tradition because sexual pleasure is expressed outside the marital relationship, with its procreative potential, and semen is not deposited in the vagina.

Moral theologians have, for some time now, mitigated the gravity of this sin on the grounds that young people are ignorant, have limited choice and do not give full consent to the evil involved. In my book, *Proposals for a New Sexual Ethic*, which is based on an early exploration of the change of sexual morality from biology to personal love, I took the view that no sin is involved in adolescent masturbation, a view which other moral theologians have also adopted independently, and nothing since then has made me change my mind. In puberty and adolescence the young person is becoming acquainted with his/her sexuality and the purpose of sexuality at that stage is to learn how to be a sexual person. Neither human development nor sexual morality envisages relationships at this time within which intercourse should take place. The young person is becoming acquainted with their sexuality and one way of doing so is through masturbation.

But while I see nothing wrong in masturbation confined to adolescence, I draw a clear line against sexual intercourse which is an act that involves another person. For, as we have seen, at the centre of adolescence is sexual discovery and the possibility of forming later sexual attachment. The fact that sexual intercourse is possible does not mean that it is meaningful in the context of this phase of life. My objection therefore is not primarily biological, although I do recognise the importance of not having a baby outside the framework of two caring and supportive parents.

My main objection is that adolescence is a time dedicated generally to independence, the discovery of a suitable alterna-

tive to parents and then finally the formation of a new attachment. It is a period when young people test each other for
mutual suitability. Sexual intercourse does not help to
discover whether a potential partner is trustworthy, reliable,
has or has not a quick temper, is capable of loving or being
loved, is caring, affectionate, a reliable worker, honest,
considerate, faithful, capable of emotional closeness, sensitive
but not over-sensitive, stable but can take initiative, disci-
plined but can enjoy life, conscientious but not rigid, flexible
but not indecisive. It takes a long time and a number of
friendships to discover a partner who is capable of establishing a lifelong relationship which is exclusive, permanent
and faithful – the characteristics of marriage for most
societies. In brief, the sexual dimension of the personality is
designed for forming an adult attachment and in this sexual
intercourse plays no part. When the attachment has been
formed, coitus is primarily concerned to maintain the bond.
This view is in keeping with the phases of human
development.

Premarital chastity has nothing therefore to do with emphasising the importance of female virginity. The idea long
current in western society that men could enjoy sexual intercourse before marriage but women had to remain chaste,
developed a dual standard of sexual morality which has no
particular merit. Premarital chastity obtains as much for the
man as for the woman. It is an ideal which has been all but
lost in recent times, and in my opinion the advent of AIDS
is an appropriate time for its reconsideration. Let us now
consider the arguments which have been offered in favour of
premarital intercourse.

First, as already mentioned, there are those who say there
is no connection between intercourse and a personal relationship. Sex is for pleasure only. This argument is favoured more
by men than women. But the contention is simply not true.
We have seen that from the first year of life instincts are
integrated in the whole personality; they do not live as
separate entities and they have been shaped and controlled
in an interaction with parents who relate in love. Thus to

63

separate sex from the rest of the personality and to isolate it from feelings is a distortion of authentic human encounters. When coitus takes place there is a meeting of persons (not just a union of genitals), with the integrity of feelings and emotions involved.

Closely following on this argument has to be the repudiation of the biological statement, that now that contraception is available there is no risk to new life. Apart from the fact that the facilitation of fornication has not been matched by an equivalent use of contraceptives, the case against premarital intercourse should not be primarily biological, although that is important. The issue is that sexual intercourse by itself should not be the means of discovering the suitability of a relationship, but rather should seal the relationship when an apt choice has been made.

We cannot stress too much that adolescence is a time for sexual attachment which needs testing through companionship. Coitus is not a research tool for personal compatibility, but later completes the compatibility that has already been achieved.

Another facile argument is that sexual compatibility is of paramount importance in permanent relationships and as such should be tested before marriage. In practice sexual affinity and fulfilment follow closely or from personal amiability. When the relationship is good sex is often good; furthermore when the relationship is stable and satisfactory it can compensate for poor or even absent sex. In other words the key to satisfactory sex is satisfactory relationship. Premarital sex, however good, is rarely an indication of how the relationship will turn out. Whereas the establishment of sound personal relationship is the best guarantee for marital stability and successful intercourse.

Even when these considerations are conceded it is still held that it is impossible to remain chaste before marriage. For myself and millions of my own generation who observed the rule of premarital chastity, the idea that instincts are so overwhelming that they cannot be contained is novel. There is no doubt that the relevant factor here is the attitude of society and of the individual. If society takes the view that restraint is not possible and indeed bombards the young person with sexual titillation and condoms, then clearly society is of no assistance whatsoever in sexual control. When Christianity attempts to obtain control by negation and inhibition in sexual matters it loses credence and young people simply rebel against it. What is needed is a combination of positive and welcoming acceptance of sexuality and at the same time a code of discipline, based on human development, which sees sexuality as a particularly rich and significant experience whose full meaning can only be realised in the context of a permanent, committed and faithful relationship, signifying the full donation of one person to another in a relationship of love. There is no doubt that men and women are perfectly capable of making a whole range of sacrifices when these are needed and seen clearly to be appropriate. Sex is precious when used in the right way but when it is misused it loses its worth and value, and at the moment society is debasing the sexual currency.

Summary

Traditionally both society and Christianity saw the beginning of sexuality at puberty. This is a fundamental mistake. Sexuality is part of the whole person and is embedded in the human personality from the time of birth. From that moment onwards instincts play a vital part in the growth of the personality, are part of its basic goodness, and are integrated in the whole person in the context of the growth of a loving relationship with the parents.

Before puberty the young person acquired a mass of characteristics which play a vital part in loving personal relationships and become essential in the maintenance of love between two adults. After puberty the adolescent is armed with the potential for genital activity and the desire to seek sexual relationships. The search for suitable relationship is essentially a process of personal discovery in which sexual intercourse plays no part. Coitus is not designed for the discernment of personal suitability, for it has a unique capacity of *affirming* personal choice and is a powerful means of *sealing* relationships.

Thus human sexuality is a God-given gift for differentiating between and attracting the sexes. It is the most powerful reason for forming human attachments and becomes the single most important way of confirming and maintaining the established bonds.

The present campaign against AIDS is fundamentally misconceived because its underlying assumptions about human sexuality are wrong and it is likely to end up with the same failure as the belief that the supposed availability of premarital contraception will prevent conception. The emphasis on condoms is mistaken because it relies on means rather than principles and does nothing to remove the mistaken notion that premarital sexual intercourse has the same value and validity as within marriage.

Given that premarital intercourse basically goes against the design of human development, does that mean that all such intercourse has the same meaning? This is a highly pertinent question in the current debate.

6

Premarital Intercourse

Sexual intercourse is accompanied by a number of possibilities. It is an act marked by pronounced sexual and physical excitation which, when consummated in an orgasm, gives intense pleasure and relief of the accompanying tension. When penis-vagina penetration occurs the depositing of semen in the vagina, and hence procreation, becomes a possibility. Finally there is the possibility of a personal encounter between a man and a woman possessing the dimension of love. This has been interpreted in the western tradition as having the characteristics of commitment, permanency and faithfulness. In psychological terms when people make love they feel that the genital activity becomes a language which speaks of a personal dimension of love. Genital unity becomes the symbol of personal donation in which two people feel that they receive each other wholly and in a committed manner. They are saying with sex: 'I recognise you as the most important person in my life; I want you as the most important person in my life and I appreciate you as the most important person in my life.' When these personal overtones are separated from coitus human integrity is distorted.

What sexual morality aims to achieve is an authentic expression of all the potential latent within the act of sexual intercourse. The pleasure is intrinsic to the act and its authenticity needs to be guaranteed by the attitude society and religion adopt towards it. It is Christianity that has held the greatest reservation about this pleasure, equating it for a long time with animal instinct. In this respect Christianity has been wrong. The pleasure is an essential part of the goodness of the act and is a gift from God, specially designed for human attraction and bonding. It should be cherished and celebrated, as the scriptures do in the Song of Songs.

Then there is the procreation potential of intercourse. The Roman Catholic Church, as we have seen, takes the most rigorous approach in preserving this potential by insisting that every act of coitus should be open to life, forbidding all forms of contraception.

Finally there is the distinctly human characteristic of the meeting of persons through coitus in which the act becomes a symbol of love, hence the use of the words 'making love' to describe sexual intercourse. If a society is to do justice to its sexual life it has to draw a hierarchy of values embracing these three potentials of sexual intercourse, trying then to persuade its citizens to adhere as far as possible to these values, which are consistent with basic human integrity.

The highest value in the hierarchy must be the personal dimension. In so far as coitus delivers a message of personal love the possibility will be there on each occasion, that the two human beings involved deepen their significance and attachment for one another. The personal dimension is the indispensable quality of human sexual intercourse and in Christian terms reflects a personal encounter in a relationship of love, which reflects what we know about the Trinity as a unity of persons encountering each other in love. Personal love is the highest value to be preserved.

The second value is the procreative ability of the act. Clearly it is on this potential that the world depends for its continuity. But, as I shall argue in Chapter 8 on marriage, this is a characteristic that is present over a whole lifetime of fertility and there is overwhelming evidence that the human design does not reflect a divine will that demands openness to procreation in every sexual act. So, for me, contraception in principle can be used to safeguard the higher value of personal love.

The third value is the realisation of pleasure. Here the act is pursued entirely for hedonistic purposes, the achievement of an orgasm, and the personal and procreative characteristics

68

are ignored. The pull towards hedonism is extremely powerful and there is no doubt that the advent of contraception has facilitated it. But the answer is not to condemn sexual pleasure or contraception but to educate young people towards the personal meaning of coitus.

In this context some might argue that the hierarchy of values outlined is not comprehensive. There are other values which lead to casual sex. The first is the recognition of intercourse as a symbol of maturity. Children do not have sexual intercourse but adults do. Thus the adolescent who has sex is led to believe that he or she has arrived. Young men and women are pressurised to have intercourse as a sign of adulthood, for they can boast afterwards that they have had sex, thus hoping to gain respect and recognition. This is a great temptation but one that fails the test of human integrity, for the act is much more than a social marker. There are plenty of these to indicate the transition from childhood to adulthood, as we discussed in Chapter 5 (p. 60). But what is not realised by those who advocate coitus as a sign of adulthood is that psychologically coitus carries with it an intense degree of exclusivity. It is felt as a most powerful personal sign of 'this man' or 'this woman' making love to 'me'. It is therefore quite inappropriate that it should become an occasion for social achievement.

The next argument used, particularly by young men, is that coitus is a sign of conquest, in particular of male conquest. This is the image of man as the hunter who sets out to search and overcome the female. This view of 'machismo', or male superiority, may have had a place in the annals of evolution but within the context of the equality of dignity between the sexes, it certainly does not.

Another reason is that the girl offers herself for intercourse as a payment for the attention received from the boy. It is expected and, if not delivered, the boy looks elsewhere. The answer here is that there are a number of other ways of appreciating an evening out, and intercourse, with its rich personal meaning, is inappropriate as a way of saying thanks.

A further contention is that, while sexual intercourse

undoubtedly has a personal dimension, this value is not so high or exclusive as it is made out to be. The act does no more than show interest in another person and carries no significance of permanency, exclusiveness or faithfulness. There is no doubt that men and women look at coitus differently, although there are exceptions. Men tend to emphasise the physical dimension and minimise the personal one. For them the pleasure of orgasm – which is almost inevitably present – signifies a shared experience of momentary togetherness which needs no past or future. It is love for the occasion. The woman may or may not experience an orgasm. For her the man's giving of himself takes on a more personal meaning and is linked with attachment and affection. For her coitus can certainly be enjoyed at the physical level, but it is a more distinctly personal experience which anticipates continuity, reliability and predictability. There is little doubt then that casual sex is more in tune with male than female psychology. Women are much more aware of their potential creativity and of the need to establish a lasting and secure relationship, although these differences between the sexes are open to many exceptions. Thus there are women who claim to enjoy casual sex and men who seek for more attachment through it. The point to be made is that intrinsic in the sexual act is the tendency for attachment in and through the personal encounter and, when this dimension is ignored, then the meaning of the act is devalued.

From the foregoing discussion it can be seen that the meaning and morality of sexual intercourse varies according to the circumstances in which it is carried out. The traditional Christian view is that all premarital sexual intercourse can be dismissed as fornication. It cannot.

There is a marked difference between coitus carried out casually and that which occurs between a committed couple who are living in an exclusive and faithful relationship. This distinction is made increasingly and the apparent lack of any differentiation in Christian thought between the two varieties of intercourse can only be seen as a handicap. Recent writings by moral theologians however are beginning to reflect the difference. In my *Proposals for a New Sexual Ethic* I pointed to a spectrum of premarital sexual intercourse ranging from casual sex with a prostitute to having intercourse with one's fiancée the night before the wedding. Anyone can see there is a difference.

Casual Sex

Those who advocate sex for pleasure, or for any of the other reasons mentioned, are trying to persuade society that sex in all these different circumstances is valid and justified. In the course of the analysis made in this chapter it clearly is not. In brief, sexual intercourse has three dimensions of pleasure: release of physiological tension, procreation and a personal encounter of love. The persistent attempt to ignore the second and, in particular, the third dimension is clearly an attempt to pervert human values.

From time immemorial attempts have been made to make coitus solely a pleasure-giving encounter; the fact that such a view has never completely prevailed is an enduring manifestation of the conviction that there is more to sexual intercourse than pleasure. While I part company with making procreation an indispensable value, it is clear beyond any shadow of doubt that pleasure alone is an insufficient expression of the potential of coitus. In its human aspects the act is a symbol and a promise of unity, availability, affection, personal donation, which are such rich characteristics that they need the appropriate features of continuity, reliability and predictability, conditions which pertain to marriage, to realise their full potential.

The AIDS campaign, as mentioned, recognises that casual sex, which implies multiple sexual encounters, is a risk to health and as such is persistently advising the use of condoms. But this advice is an incomplete answer from society and as such there is a grave failure of responsibility towards its citizens. There *is* an urgent need for a campaign of education in the media, in schools and in the home, which teaches the meaning of sexuality. The government is naive to take the view that the arrival of AIDS can be handled in isolation from fundamental human and moral attitudes to casual sex.

Premarital Coitus

One of the most frequent questions I am asked when I lecture is that of the status of cohabitation. Both cohabitation and premarital intercourse have been rising in western societies. Thus in one British study the proportion of women who first married in 1956–60, 1961–5, 1966–70 and 1971–5 reported an incidence of premarital sexual intercourse of 35, 47, 61 and 74 per cent respectively. The proportion of women who lived with their husband before marriage was 1, 3, 3 and 9 per cent respectively. The period of reported premarital cohabitation was fairly short: 26 per cent reported a duration of less than three months; 15 per cent between three and five months and 24 per cent more than six months but less than a year. Thus nearly two-thirds of those who lived with their husbands before marriage had done so for less than a year, some 20 per cent between one and two years and the remaining 15 per cent for two years or longer.

Clearly a new pattern of behaviour has emerged, especially during the last decade, for which there are various explanations. Those who take a condemnatory attitude to all that has happened in the last quarter of a century may assume that this increase of premarital intercourse and cohabitation is another indication of the moral depravity of our age. Others may see it as a consequence of housing difficulties and economic reason; but that is not the whole explanation for a phenomenon seen in many western countries.

While it is possible that the greater latitude shown towards sexual intercourse has been extended to include premarital intercourse, cohabitation appears to me to be a distinct effort on the part of young people to take precautions against marital breakdown by getting to know each other well before marriage. This is an understandable step, for society has done nothing to stem the rising tide of divorce. Whether cohabitation is the answer to divorce is a different matter.

The factors contributing to marital breakdown are many and diverse and cannot always be anticipated. But final opinion must be suspended until widespread studies show whether there is any difference in rates of breakdown between those who have cohabited and those who have not.

If we return to the morality of premarital intercourse, there is a clear difference between casual sex and that which occurs between those committed to a permanent, faithful and exclusive relationship. These are the conditions which nurture the personal dimensions of coitus and therefore the most crucial human value is preserved. This leads to other questions frequently posed by young people: 'Why should I bother to marry at all? What is a ceremony going to add to the love which I now experience without marriage?'

Both in respect of the marriage ceremony and of premarital intercourse it has to be said that circumstances do alter; promises and even engagements are broken. The principal point to be made is that, just as there is a spectrum of human sexuality between the casual and the committed, there is a range of human commitment varying from promise to vows. A promise is not a vow, which realises the deepest elements of human truth.

Even more important is the social dimension of the wedding ceremony, of love, commitment, unity, of having a child and raising it. We all need more than a personal encounter, for in every one of us there is an essential social dimension. The decision to relate permanently to another human being in love and raise a family is as much a social as a personal statement and needs the involvement and the support of society. In fact a great deal of married life (such as: what are the duties and obligations of spouses to one another; or, how is their property shared and to whom does it belong), has a social dimension as is readily seen when marriages break down.

A wedding ceremony, with witnesses from the community, acts as a guarantee of the personal love between spouses. In Christian terms the marriage is considered to be a sacrament, but even then it is not the minister who administers it but the couple, one to another. The priest and the witnesses are representatives of church and society, present to give the religious and social assent to the personal commitment of the couple.

It can thus be seen that coitus between committed persons has a much greater human authenticity, and therefore validity and integrity. But, given human frailty, the ideal is undoubtedly to place coitus within the context of a permanent, faithful and exclusive relationship which has been ratified by a wedding ceremony.

Sexual Needs

I return now to the point that will undoubtedly be raised by some critics, namely that the concept of premarital chastity is fine but no consideration is given to the reality that men and women are sexual beings with the need to obtain relief from their libidinal drive. Premarital chastity is fine when marriage takes place soon after puberty, and chastity in general is realisable when it becomes a clear goal, such as for those who take vows of celibacy.

This is a point of view that cannot be lightly dismissed. At a time when marriage is likely to last fifty years or more, as a result of increasing longevity, every study has shown that it should not be entered into until the middle twenties when a minimum social, emotional and sexual maturity has been reached. Marriages which occur before the age of twenty are distinctly more prone to breakdown than those which take place later on.

What is the answer to this criticism? No one has formulated a perfect answer although societies all over the world have tried a variety of solutions. Since the sexual pressures on the male appear to be the stronger, one solution has been to designate a group of women as prostitutes who make their bodies available for a price. These women had – and continue to have – a bad reputation but have traditionally salvaged the good name of the rest of womanhood. Such a solution bristles with objections. Why should some women feel obliged

74

to assume this role, especially for economic reasons? The answer is that women are not compelled to become prostitutes; they choose their trade freely. Yet every study of prostitution suggests that this freedom is delusory, and that women often find their way to this work for a wide variety of economic and psychological reasons in which their freedom is gravely curtailed. Like all sexual minorities this group of women and a minority of men have never received adequate consideration from society. They are used and re-used and very few care what happens to them. The union of a prostitute and her client is one of the most impoverished of human encounters and, however necessary society may find it to permit it, can never be the appropriate answer.

The next answer is a combination of avoidance of sexual intercourse, with alternative orgasmic outlets that are either spontaneous or self-induced. This solution is widely resorted to but has long had the disapproval of Christianity, which condemns masturbation as immoral. This disapproval is based on the biological grounds that sex always has a procreative dimension that is denied in masturbation. This is a view that many moral theologians no longer share and I place myself in their ranks. The combination of coital avoidance coupled with spontaneous or induced orgasm is probably one of the commonest patterns of sexual behaviour. It is far from perfect because, as we have seen, human sexual desire has an inbuilt personal dimension. Solitary sex is a diminished experience.

Thirdly there is the option of sexual abstinence. Here it is necessary to be realistic. Abstinence is neither as easy as some Christians have advocated nor as impossible as society currently accepts. There are psychological and physiological forces, which vary from person to person, driving towards orgastic release. In our society these internal pressures are aided and abetted by social sexual titillation, which is widespread. Sexual abstinence is never easy but becomes easier after consideration and when an effort is made to achieve it. It is facilitated too when the personal and loving dimension becomes the primary reason. The point I am making here is that it should be seriously considered, which is precisely what the current AIDS campaign does not do.

Summary

The prevailing view of premarital sex is, at its worst, one of hedonistic pursuit and, at its best, that each sexual occasion is one of instant and temporary bonding with no lasting or enduring meaning. Such a view permits and encourages casual sex but discourages the rich potential of sexual intercourse. This sees intercourse as a fruitful and positive act which has pleasure, procreation and love as its meaning. While pleasure and procreation are subordinate to the personal dimension, the latter is its supreme human expression. In its human dimension the sexual instinct is integrated within the whole personality and is a symbol of a loving commitment of exclusiveness, faithfulness and permanency. Through exclusiveness, a couple are promising to love one another to the exclusion of others. Through faithfulness, they are offering to love one another without fear of rejection and loss of this love to a third party. Through permanency, they are offering one another what all human beings long for and have been conditioned to in childhood, namely continuity, reliability and predictability.

In this chapter, and throughout the book, it is assumed that Christian morality simply represents human authenticity and integrity although everybody realises that it is not easy to achieve this. Christianity postulates the presence of sin, mankind's tendency to move away from God, to rebel and repudiate his love. Those who do not accept the concept of sin nevertheless accept that of human integrity, which is expressed in terms of the realisation of human potential. Whatever concept is postulated, there is little doubt that sexual integrity before marriage and, as we shall see, within marriage, is difficult to realise; but that is no reason for giving up altogether as society is currently doing.

The AIDS campaign is the epitome of despair of achieving sexual integrity and the condom has become the symbol of compromise with which it is hoped, at least, health will be maintained. Good health needs more than condoms; it requires appropriate attitudes. Sooner or later these have to be rediscovered by society.

7

Promiscuity

The knowledge we have acquired about infection with the HTLVIII/LAV virus suggests that the danger of being infected increases with frequent sexual intercourse carried out with multiple partners. That is precisely what promiscuity is. Public opinion and Christian thought have tended to associate promiscuity with the pursuit of sexual pleasure. The activity of such pleasure-seeking men and women is often compared with that of animals. Such comparison is unsatisfactory and unproductive. Human beings have a prolonged childhood in which social and emotional attachment, based on one-to-one relationships, forms their natural orientation. Unlike animals, instincts in human beings are part of the whole personality which is directed towards forming a relationship of love with another person. Any deviation from one-to-one relationships is much more than a reversion to instinctual activity. It is a distortion of the capacity to form the personal encounters psychology has helped us to understand. In this chapter I want to look at promiscuity from the social and psychological point of view and to look briefly at its consequences.

Social

In Chapter 5 I proposed that the decade between puberty and the early twenties was a time for exploring the formation of personal attachments. During this period the principal task of young people is to separate from parents, form relationships with their peers, test the suitability of, and finally form a strong bond with another person in an exclusive commitment which we call marriage. I expressed the view that sexual intercourse was not a suitable means for testing personal qualities but had the characteristics rather of *confirming* relationship.

But there are cultures which do not take this view. In Britain the West Indian tradition links adolescence and sexuality much more closely. Women often give a history of having a baby before marriage and with a man who is not subsequently the husband. Such a cultural characteristic may have resulted from the original conditions of slavery in which the loving attachment of persons was secondary to the production of more slaves. That is not to say that illegitimate births are confined to West Indians. They are not. Indigenous cultures can fall prey to premarital intercourse which is undoubtedly due to the proclivity for instant and complete attachment. The overlap between the social and the sexual is such that there is always a temptation to seek instant total unity. The desire for this unity is so powerful that couples can find themselves having intercourse without taking any contraceptive precautions, hence the point that I have made repeatedly that the principal deterrent to premarital pregnancy is not to be found in contraceptives but in the will.

In the last quarter of a century the social climate has veered towards a greater assent to premarital intercourse, so that we have a combination of social factors which have facilitated frequent and multiple sexual intercourse, that is, promiscuity.

There are also social circumstances which can lead to sexual intercourse with prostitutes or to other forms of promiscuity, for example when spouses, often men, find themselves having no access to their partner. Husbands may behave in this way when they are away from their wives or their wives are pregnant, ill or do not enjoy sex. Thus both men and women who leave their spouses for variable periods on business or to attend conferences often find themselves in circumstances of isolation and loneliness in which instant attachment, however temporary, is attractive. Those who plan such ventures ahead do so with contraceptive foresight. Offering business men sexual hospitality when abroad has become far more common in recent decades, and if the AIDS virus is found to pass from women to men this will become a dangerous method of becoming infected.

When a strong procreative theology prevailed, having intercourse during pregnancy was considered a horrifying violation of the sanctity of life and those who did so were branded as grossly immoral. As this view receded another false view arose, namely that coitus during pregnancy was capable of inducing a spontaneous abortion, thus limiting it during this period. Some women who did not enjoy sex used pregnancy as an excuse to avoid having intercourse. Lastly, natural discomfort during the later stages of pregnancy curtailed coitus. For these reasons some husbands find themselves married but with no access to a sexual partner. It is of course precisely in these circumstances that fidelity is greatly appreciated. But some men find themselves unable to abstain. This is where the local prostitute becomes available.

Another reason for the resort to prostitution is the unavailability of either spouse through illness, imprisonment or war. One of the most pervasive anxieties of prisoners while they are incarcerated is the faithfulness of their spouse.

A point of interest which arises in all these circumstances is why the partner needs to have sexual intercourse with another man or woman. If the need, as is popularly claimed, is solely the relief of sexual tension, would not masturbation do? In this apparently simple question is to be found a profound truth. However much theologians and popular fantasy proclaim the truth that all that is sought is sexual pleasure, the fact is that the meaning of coitus is much more than the resulting orgasm. Sexual attraction leading to intercourse is a desire for interpersonal contact in which the arms of another human being become the gateway to being recognised, wanted and appreciated. Intercourse is most complete when bodies become the means for personal affirmation. Thus coitus cannot be compared to animal sexuality for the desire for human contact is *so* compelling that promiscuity seems to provide an instant answer.

Psychological

In addition to social reasons, psychological ones can also give rise to promiscuity. As already described, the human infant has the capacity to form one-to-one relationships through the mechanism of attachment. Human beings are built psychologically for personal attachments whose inner qualities are inclined towards exclusivity, reliability and predictability, reflecting the exclusive relationship of child and parent.

Some men and women find it difficult to form exclusive attachments. They move from one person to another and their sexual life reflects this multiplicity. It goes without saying that such promiscuity is highly inducive to HTLVIII/LAV virus infection and is equally applicable to homosexuals and heterosexuals. For the present it is homosexual promiscuity that carries the highest risk of infection, but the psychological factors involved apply equally to both groups.

The psychological model is that of attachment theory described by Bowlby and developed by others, as outlined on page 51. Dynamic abnormal psychology has tried to describe the circumstances in which the relationship between child and parent is disturbed and the growing person does not receive an affirmative experience of being recognised, wanted and appreciated. In these circumstances a wounded personality develops which is unsure whether others want it or whether they are prepared to put up with its limitations and stand by when it is not particularly attractive or lovable. These are men and women who have what Bowlby calls 'anxious attachments'. They are constantly worried as to how they are received and expect to be rejected for the slightest reason or no reason at all.

Those who believe that homosexuality results from extremely unstable parental conditions, in which the father is distant or rejects the young girl or boy, relate the homosexual instability in personal relations in adulthood to these unpromising beginnings in childhood. Hence my own plea that the supreme objective of Christianity must be to help

81

homosexuals establish stable personal relationships which advance their capacity to love and be loved and diminish the risk of infection by the HTLVIII/LAV virus.

Bowlby describes six situations which promote anxious attachments.

The first is when one or both parents are persistently unresponsive to the child's care, actively disparaging, or when they reject him. At one extreme are to be found children who are actively abused physically and/or rejected. Such overt physical and social neglect is obviously the opposite of love; but there are many adults who describe an idyllic relationship with their parents who, on close enquiry, are found to have had nothing of the sort. These are men and women who grew up in homes where their physical and intellectual needs were met. They were fed, dressed, kept clean and tidy, sent to school where their cognitive development was observed meticulously; but when one looks at their emotional experience these men and women had no sense of being loved. Their parents were often too busy with their work or career, or were undemonstrative and did not show feelings. I have coined the term that such children were 'serviced' rather than loved. These men and women grew up competent physically and intellectually, are indeed often very intelligent and learned and have distinguished positions in society but are unable to form stable intimate relationships.

The second pattern is caused by discontinuous parenting. Children who are frequently separated from parents, sent to child carers or relatives, or spend repeated periods in hospitals or institutions, such as many children from broken homes do today, lack the opportunity of having stable and continuous relationships with key figures who love them.

The third cause is the persistent threat from parents not to love the child, used as a means of controlling him. This is a discipline of despair in which often mother – but sometimes father – tries to elicit obedience on the basis of withdrawing love if the child does not comply with their wishes. This is conditional love, which is far more widespread than at first appears. It is an elementary conditioning in which the immature inept parent has no other way of controlling the child than the threat of withdrawing love. It is a golden rule that every child needs unconditional love, which is never withdrawn however much its behaviour is disapproved.

The fourth mechanism which can cause anxious attachments in later life is the threat of parents to abandon the family, used either as a method of disciplining the child or of influencing the spouse. Once again this is a common disturbance pattern in which the parent, particularly the mother, is constantly saying she will leave home if her wishes are not met. The child then lives with the constant threat of being abandoned. The overheard arguments between parents are a regular occasion for the return of the terror that the next day the household will be left with only one parent. Such childhoods are laden with terror which continue in adult life.

The fifth possibility is a variant of the fourth, when the parent threatens to desert, kill their partner or commit suicide. The young child, living in an atmosphere of such constant possible loss, is experiencing the peak of instability. It is often too young to realise that the difficulty lies within the parent and may feel guilty or bad for what is happening to the parent.

The sixth set of circumstances are those in which a child is made to feel guilty by denouncing his behaviour as being responsible for the parent's illness or death.

In all these circumstances the child not only lacks steady and reliable signals of recognition, acceptance and appreciation but is often made overtly, or latently, to feel guilty for the damage done to the parents. It is not surprising if, as a result, a number of adverse features develop in its own personality.

The adult who has experienced such a childhood does not feel accepted, wanted or desired. Sexual intercourse is carried out with people who have no significance for them. Nobody can love them, so coitus becomes a physical event with no emotional dimension or personal overtones. Partners are changed and treated as objects. Another result is the grown up man or woman who does not trust anyone, so no intimate relationship is ever established. Others are used for sexual relief but their own person is never entrusted to them.

A childhood of the type described may lead to an excessive sensitivity in which they feel easily criticised and rejected. Under these conditions they may have intercourse with people who do not matter, often men or women who are socially and intellectually inferior, whose opinion or approval is irrelevant. One is beyond criticism in their presence.

Another reaction to such an unhappy childhood is to feel extremely angry. This is an anger which seeks to humiliate, hurt and attack others as sexual objects. The small group of sexual murderers may have such a background.

It is clear that such a precarious childhood leads to a lot of insecurity about one's worth. Such men and women seek many sexual experiences, always hoping that the next one will provide the definitive answer to their feelings of acceptance. But the reassurance is short-lived and very soon they are once again seeking evidence of being wanted. Such anxious attachments and their consequences form the background of the army of men and women who have multiple and frequent sexual contacts to overcome their anxieties about being recognised as significant, wanted and appreciated. They contribute significantly to promiscuity. Anxious attachment is a major problem for homosexuality.

Of course the promiscuous group I am describing lies at the extremity of psychological wounding. Some men and women with 'anxious attachment' personalities do form exclusive marital relationships and then experience their fears of being unloved and unwanted within the relationship. As we shall see later these problems often contribute to marital infidelity.

There are two other personality types associated with unstable sexual experiences. The first is that of the schizoid, a man or woman whose emotions are flat, who has very little affectivity and is cold and distant. Such men and women find it difficult to relate to others and have impersonal sexual contacts which are largely directed towards the relief of sexual needs.

84

Connected with the above group are to be found men and women, but particularly the former, who are physically or socially unacceptable. These men feel totally unable to approach women socially for sexual relations and resort to prostitutes, whom they feel will be able to relate to their limitations.

Finally there are two further links between promiscuity and personality. In the school of thought of behaviourism the human personality is largely shaped by biological genetic factors which influence the part of the brain called the cortex. In this theoretical world men and women are divided into extroverts, introverts and neurotics (those prone to extreme anxiety). According to H. J. Eysenck extroverts have problems with learning, retaining and sensitisation, needing repeated sensory stimuli for excitation. Eysenck provides evidence that extroverts on the whole require much greater sexual stimulation than introverts and are more likely to fall into promiscuous behaviour, if other circumstances conducive to a stable relationship are not present.

Psychiatrists and psychologists are very fond of using the term 'psychopath' to denote another group of men and women who are socially and emotionally unstable, unreliable and aggressive, who form poor relationships, and are often to be found in promiscuous, alcoholic and drug-addiction groups. Although the term 'psychopath' is widely used, the men and women who come under this category form a heterogeneous collection in which anxiety, anxious attachment, emotional instability, moodiness and aggressiveness are present in excess, making social and emotional stability very difficult.

In this section I have tried to show that there is a psychological category of promiscuity and that it is a complex phenomenon without easy solutions. There is no doubt that both prostitutes and their clients often possess a large element of this dimension of psychological disturbance. Thus while society and Christianity can advocate social and will-power control over sexual behaviour, some men and women are not free emotionally to obey the instructions of either. These people need a lot of help to overcome their difficulties.

Consequences of Promiscuity

There are some who put forward the view that sexual intercourse is a harmless and pleasurable experience whose only objective must be quantity, as often as possible with as many people as will consent. This philosophy has attracted much attention in recent decades and I want to end this chapter by pointing out that the consequences of promiscuity are anything *but* harmless.

Of the social implications, the first and most serious is that indiscriminate sex leads to pregnancies in which children are born in adverse circumstances and grow up in inimical social and psychological situations. The alternative is abortion and the acceptability of such killing is one of the blights of our contemporary society. The easing of conditions for coitus, at the crudest level, releases unacceptable drives which lead to rape. At another level women feel coerced to agree to sexual intercourse when they are neither inclined nor want to participate, simply to feel socially accepted. This leads to coitus becoming a game with men and women as pawns or objects with all the resultant trivialisation.

Secondly there are adverse physical consequences. Those who participate in promiscuous sexual behaviour are more prone to become infected with HTLVIII/LAV and to catch venereal disease. It is true that venereal disease can be treated but it is much more easily identified in men than women. It can damage women's capacity to become fertile as their Fallopian tubes become infected and blocked. There is also evidence that cancer of the cervix is associated with promiscuous behaviour.

Thirdly and most subtly, the presence of promiscuity gives rise to a sinister devaluation of human meaning. Coitus is an act between the sexes which, as I shall show in Chapter 8, carries a rich range of personal meanings. Beyond its pleasurable and procreative significance, it can express a powerful dimension of love. When this is removed what is left is only an animal residue. Even worse, when coitus is emptied of its loving meaning, a vacuum of cynicism, emptiness and loss

86

of meaning is created. Sex then becomes a physical entity, bargaining for favours, money or some advantage; such devaluation continues too in permanent relationships. The whole of society therefore is impoverished when the richness of coitus is minimised.

The moral consequences are based on the social, physical and psychological ones. Human beings are created in the image of God with the potential of loving and when that possibility is reduced, everybody suffers. The opposite characteristics which emerge are mistrust, lower expectations, destabilisation of relationships and, above all, the impoverishment of the potential of one of the most meaningful human acts.

8

Sex within Marriage

It has been argued that coitus is not appropriate during the decade of separation from parents, concluding in the early twenties, when a final choice is made of establishing a permanent relationship called marriage, within which children are born and reared and the spouses grow and develop over a possible span of over fifty years of life. Within the context of marriage, that is, in an established relationship, the value of coitus is to be found in its ability to maintain the relationship.

Before examining the capacities of coitus to maintain a bond, a brief reference has to be made to the permanent relationship we call marriage. Marriage and the family are institutions with ubiquitous presence proclaiming something basic about human nature. Sociologists will claim that the family is necessary for the birth and raising of the next generation and the mutual support of the spouses. Psychologists would argue that in fact human beings are programmed to form relationships based on attachment and that marriage is the adult equivalent of the childhood bonds between child and parent.

This is not the place to discuss in detail why marriage and the family are such basic ingredients of humanity, but it is important to note that alternatives have always been suggested. While everyone agrees that couples are needed to have children, it has been postulated that children can be raised by the state, thus eliminating the need for the family. Such alternatives have never found favour and even the kibbutz accepts an increasing involvement of parents in the care of their children.

Thus having and raising a family is one of the basic reasons for marriage; but not the sole reason. The human propensity for attachment means that a close relationship is the norm for optimum realisation of human potential. Once again it would need a whole book to consider in detail why human beings need intimacy and exclusivity to thrive. But here it is sufficient to note that since time immemorial marriage and the family have provided the conditions for the continuity of the race. In the West today the duration of marriage has increased considerably, placing a great strain on the permanency of the relationship. Considerable advances in medicine have made pregnancy reliable and predictable and have meant that women do not have to spend a major part of their life in procreation. An increasing understanding of the dignity of life has shifted emphasis from numbers of children to the quality of their lives and the size of the family has been gradually reduced. In addition the advent of widespread and effective contraception has made conception a deliberate and planned activity, allowing the desired family size to be achieved with the minimum of sexual activity, leaving the major part of sexual intercourse free from procreation. This liberation of coitus from its procreative intent is also realised by Roman Catholics who use the infertile period method. Thus for the whole of western society, and increasingly for the rest of humanity, a point has been reached when the overwhelming majority of sexual intercourse is knowingly, consciously and deliberately non-procreative. This transformation is a basic challenge to a world that has linked coitus with procreation ever since the dawn of time. For me this is one of the most basic questions of our age. If the main reason for sexual intercourse is not procreation then what is its meaning? Has it got any value other than providing sexual pleasure? One of my greatest concerns (discussed in Chapter 3) is that this question has been largely ignored by society and by Christianity.

The absence of a coherent answer as to the non-procreative value of sexual intercourse has been the single most important reason for the ascendancy of hedonism and the indifference shown to the Christian teaching of chastity. Men and women know intuitively that coitus has other values and have looked in vain to Christianity for a lead. I consider the answer to this question to be fundamental for society and Christianity and, as far as my own Roman Catholic Church is concerned, far more important than whether every sexual act should be open to life, the argument which has preoccupied the Catholic Church for the last twenty years.

In this chapter I offer an outline of the answer to the meaning of coitus beyond its procreative potential. I do not imply that my suggestions are exhaustive but they do point to an inner world of richness reinforcing the widespread conviction that sex offers far more than pleasure and procreation, and recalling far more fundamental reasons for the pursuit of chastity, which for me is the attempt to safeguard all the potential characteristics of sexual intercourse.

Attachment

Medieval moralists in particular, following a long tradition of comparing human to animal behaviour, saw fertility as the common link. Even within this line of thought the view is fundamentally wrong. The prime purpose of sexuality, so clear in humanity, is to form pairing: the formation and maintenance of attachment which then allows for procreation. Without attachment there would be no marriage, which precedes procreation. So in searching for the fundamental meaning of sexual attraction we find it in the facilitation of human bonds between men and women, and thereafter in their maintenance through sexual intercourse. It can be argued that human bonds are found not only through sexual attraction but through sibship and friendship. That is perfectly true; but looking at the overall human situation one cannot help reaching the conclusion that the fundamental unit of society is the man-woman relationship of marriage and the family, from which spring the wider possibilities of attachment. Sexual attraction and intercourse have as their principal meaning then the unity of the sexes. The search for the fundamental value of coitus has to be directed at its capacity to maintain the man-woman relationship. How does it do this?

Body Language

Sexual intercourse is an intimate encounter of bodies in which the genitalia play a pertinent part but at the same time the act involves whole persons. When persons meet in such intimacy they give messages to each other. Sexual intercourse is a specific act which occurs within the context of a continuous relationship. It is not just a meeting of genitalia but of persons with a past and a future. The whole experience, with its accompanying intense pleasure, becomes a body language in which the sexual components become the means of reaching and addressing each other. The language is rich and the challenge is to decode its messages. What are husbands and wives saying to each other?

Feelings

The first point is that a couple make love against a background of feelings about themselves and each other. The first feeling is that of sexual arousal. Here men are more often sexually aroused when they approach their wives than their spouse who often needs tenderness, affection and sexual stimulation to become as ready as their husband. Such mutual arousal needs awareness, discipline and sustained gentle effort to bring each other to a high pitch of sexual readiness for penetration. The husband, who is often more aroused, does not always remember to prepare his wife adequately for intercourse. So an element of selfishness can enter from the very beginning of the act.

The second range of feelings is the state of the spouses who may be relaxed, tense, irritable, tired, in pain or not interested in sex at all. A positive response to the overtures of their spouse may often involve overcoming a whole range of feelings which are opposed to having sex. Here effort, sacrifice and

91

love come into operation as a man or woman shifts from inhibition to sexual assent.

Thirdly the couple have feelings for each other. This is particularly true of the wife, for whom the desirability of sexual intercourse is often placed in the context of the quality of the prevailing relationship, and in particular what has transpired between the spouses during the preceding twenty-four hours. It is self-evident that there is an intimate connection between the feeling atmosphere in the couple's life and the consummation of sex. In this respect there is a gradual reconciliation over time between the different needs of the couple. The husband's approach to sexual intercourse is largely influenced by physical needs and the wife's by her overall feeling state, although there is a good deal of overlap between the two. In due course men have to learn to pay more attention to the wife's feelings and women to their husband's physical needs. This is a reorientation which takes place over time and is one of the several reasons that sexual intercourse naturally belongs to a continuous relationship.

Personal Affirmation

When a married couple agree to have sex, they are assenting to a great deal more than just to unite genitally. They are making themselves totally available, body, mind and feelings and are thus indicating an enormous degree of acceptance of each other. Human beings have a whole range of possibilities with which they indicate approval of each other. People smile, shake hands, agree about things, share, co-operate, give things to each other; but the greatest donation we have to offer is the whole of ourselves and that is precisely what happens at the moment of intercourse. Coitus demands a total surrender of ourselves to another person and has become a symbol of total availability of love to another person. There is nothing more of ourselves left to offer.

People make this extremely generous donation of themselves when they receive a signal which invites them to become the most important person in the life of another human being. When couples make love they signify to one another that they recognise, want and appreciate each other as the most important person in their life. The sensual excitation, intromission and friction leading to the orgasm are powerful physical commitments to give the maximum significance to the personal encounter. Spouses come to the end of intercourse with their whole body involved in a mutual surrender which has spelt out that they are the most significant person in each other's life. Coitus has thus the capacity for a personal affirmation of immense proportions.

It is this affirmation which is diminished in casual intercourse because the couple in these circumstances do not have such meaning for each other. They are often strangers who have no personal significance. Since coitus cannot by itself give them enough meaning its significance is confined to its orgastic possibilities. This is the inverse of the potential meaning of the act. In reality the physical component becomes the basis for reinforcing the personal meaning of the couple.

That is not to say that such rich involvement is always present in the life of married couples. Clearly husbands and wives are in various stages of awareness of each other. What I am suggesting is that their free consent to intercourse implies a degree of mutuality which is always reinforced.

This advance in personal significance grows as the relationship deepens and then sexual intercourse becomes the means of strengthening the attachment. This personal significance is non-existent in casual relationships, as mentioned before, and develops only as the couple become more important to each other. The richest realisation of the potential for personal affirmation comes about in those circumstances when a couple have the greatest meaning for one another, which is achieved when they have decided to commit themselves fully in marriage. What comes first is the attachment: when the attachment is forged intercourse sustains and deepens it. Thus in the presence of a loving relationship sexual intercourse becomes a symbol which signifies and achieves the unity of the couple.

93

Reconciliation

This unity of the married couple is constantly open to misunderstanding, conflict, anger and alienation. Couples argue, quarrel, feel hurt and are rejected by one another. The idyllic marriage which has no alienation is a dream that does not exist in reality. Most of the conflict between husband and wife is resolved quickly. Spouses apologise to one another and this is followed by forgiveness and reconciliation.

But sometimes the pain caused by one another is much deeper and is not easily forgiven or forgotten. At these times the couple become estranged. They are angry with each other and the first thing that suffers is their sexual relationship. If sexual intercourse was a mere physical entity it could be indulged in whatever the mood or feelings of the couple; but it is not. It is a meeting between persons with its own language. In these unresolved circumstances the language is of anger, and the desire is to punish rather than to please.

This state of tension can continue for days, weeks or even months when the couple are separated from each other by hostility. Then they decide, despite their estrangement, to make love. They may agree to have intercourse out of care, concern or compassion, even if they are still hurt and feel rejected. And then a miracle takes place. After intercourse they are no longer estranged. The act, with its powerful affirmative characteristics, has the capacity to heal the rift between them. Spouses emerge from sexual intercourse affirmed and reunited, so that they are lovers once again. Thus, beyond the capacity for personal affirmation, coitus is capable of bringing about reconciliation.

Sexual Affirmation

In the course of sexual intercourse couples caress the sexual parts of their bodies. The husband is aroused by his wife's breasts and other parts of her body and she by his physical contours. This is an exchange of sexual recognition in which the husband appreciates the feminine qualities of his wife and

94

she in turn his male characteristics. In this way couples confirm in each other their sexual identities.

These sexual characteristics carry the credentials of each other's total identity. Their manhood and womanhood stand for their whole self, and so coitus becomes a moment of immense intensity when their personhood is recognised through their sexual features.

The importance of this mutual sexual recognition is expressed in the time, effort and money spent in personal adornment. Male theologians have tended to dismiss this preoccupation as mere vanity, particularly where it concerns women. But this universal concern is far more than vanity. It is one of the most important ways that our identity is formed.

Every time we make love and find each other's bodies stimulating and pleasurable we affirm the sexual significance of each other, and through the sexual dimension our person-hood. This affirmation of the whole person becomes increas-ingly significant as we grow older and we lose our sexual attraction. In remaining faithful to each other we not only continue to give encouragement and meaning to the sexuality of our partner, but we go on reassuring them that we desire and need them as the most important person in our life. This continuity of acceptance contrasts with transient sex when we pick up and drop sexual partners as our fancy takes us. In the process of such rapid change we offer recognition one moment and rejection the next. It is not surprising that in order to minimise this hurt men and women devalue the whole of sex and strip it of its personal characteristics. As a pure leisure-time activity it no longer matters with whom one has sex, because its meaning of personal and sexual affirm-ation has been removed.

Hope

Continuing with the personal meaning of sexual intercourse in marriage, we come next to its characteristic of repetition. The frequency with which intercourse is desired is much more than a response to physiological sexual needs. Human beings are far more than animals and are capable of controlling mere instinctual drives.

Couples who are in love with one another want to make love frequently. Every pleasurable sexual act stimulates the desire for repetition the same night, the next day, the day or week after. Built within coitus is the wish for an extension of the joy experienced. Essential to this characteristic is the presence of hope that our partner will continue to love us and in this way accept us for further acts of intercourse. Thus, coitus plays a vital part in the continuity of our acceptance as a lovable person.

The desire for frequent sexual intercourse is not confined to marriage. It can also be the mark of promiscuity. In the case of the latter there is no expectation that we will continue to be meaningful to the same person over time. Coitus does indeed become a discharge of sexual energy, often coupled with an unrecognised inner despair of remaining continuously important to the same person. Hence the necessity for a variety of persons.

Within marriage this hope of repeated intercourse fades and disappears when we are no longer interested in our partner. There is no more convincing evidence of the personal significance of sex than the gradual disappearance of the desire to have intercourse, when the partner has ceased to have personal meaning. Then hope is replaced by indifference.

Thanksgiving

When a couple make love they usually experience a peak of sexual joy. Each has become the channel of intense pleasure to the other. The consequences are that in the aftermath there is a desire to express thanksgiving. Such thanksgiving can be done verbally but it is more usual to translate it in the physical dimension of lying in each other's arms and enjoying the presence of the other. It is a time of pleasurable exhaustion in which gratitude is expressed by the complete and alert awareness of the source of such delight.

Against this desire to express gratitude and thanksgiving to someone well known to us, we need to contrast the encounter of strangers, who, having become the means of mutual orgasm, have no other meaning for one another. All the desire to rejoice with the partner is stifled by the distance that divides the participants of casual sex.

Marriage and the Church

By describing the characteristics of personal and sexual affirmation, reconciliation, hope and thanksgiving I have described a range of characteristics of intercourse which can only be realised to the full in a relationship which has the continuity, reliability and predictability of marriage and contrasts sharply with the transience, shallowness and inconsistencies of casual sex.

But in describing these qualities of sex I am also trying to show that, to be revealed, this inner world of richness needs marriage. And it is the revelation of the inner meaning of coitus that is singularly absent from ecclesiastical pronouncements written, ultimately in the Roman Catholic tradition, by celibates. This is not a criticism of celibacy; but it is a world far removed from that of marriage, and the insights of celibacy, however rich, rely on intellectual abstractions which have no intimate connection with the reality of married life. It is this feeling that official documents speak about married life from the outside that makes married Catholics concerned as to whether their conjugal experiences can be really grasped. That is not to say that the church is not aware of the link between sexuality and love. It is, as the following passage from Familiaris Consortio shows:

> Consequently, sexuality, by means of which man and woman give themselves to one another through the acts which are proper and exclusive to spouses, is by no means something purely biological, but concerns the innermost

97

being of the human person as such. It is realised in a truly human way only if it is an integral part of the love by which a man and a woman commit themselves totally to one another until death. The total physical self-giving would be a lie if it were not the sign and growth of a total personal self-giving, in which the whole person – including the temporal dimension – is present.

The trouble with such a statement, examples of which abound in Familiaris-Consortio, is that the sentiment is right but the language is wrong. What married men and women need is an accurate description of their love, not in theoretical terms of its possibilities, but in a language and a manner which reveals and illuminates their experiences. This has to be a language which uses psychology, which is the nearest efficient tool we have of reaching the contemporary understanding of love.

In criticising the last important document from the Roman Catholic Church on the family, I am not suggesting that other churches have been more successful in capturing the essence of sexual intercourse. It is because the matter is so important and so urgent that I am urging a repeated return to this crucial human activity, particularly at a time when there is a need for a new moral initiative.

At the centre of sexual morality today is (as already mentioned) the critical advance from a conceptualisation which is ultimately based on biology to that which captures the mystery of love. Men and women have to be persuaded that intercourse confined to marriage really realises the richest potential of its possibility. That means that we have to unravel its deepest personal significance, which requires us to tap the experiences of married couples and invite them to offer the fruits of their understanding to the whole Christian community. As far as the Roman Catholic Church is concerned this will not be realised by appointing to church institutes concerned with the family only married men and women who are compliant with the authoritarian teaching of the church. While obedience is an excellent quality, it is not the sole arbiter or guarantee of the truth.

Contraception

It will have become abundantly clear by now that I dissent from the official teaching of the Roman Catholic Church on contraception. I do this with intense regret and with a total absence of any desire to rebel. I am well aware that some faithful Catholics, who may not be interested in the details of the argument, are extremely bothered to know how the church can possibly be wrong in such a fundamental matter, and are concerned about its credibility in its teaching on faith and morals. This concerns me as much. This is not the place to discuss the details of the church's infallibility. It is sufficient to say that the 'clear theological consensus today maintains that in the area of morality the magisterium has never exercised its official teaching authority in an infallible way by means of any solemn definition issued either by a pope or by the college of bishops gathered together in an ecumenical council' (V.J. Genovesi, SJ, *In Pursuit of Love*). The ban on contraceptives belongs to the category of authentic fallible church teachings and that means that responsible dissent is a duty for those Catholics who, in conscience, believe that the church must ultimately develop its teaching further.

That the church does in fact change its pronouncements is clear for anyone to see who has studied its theology of marriage closely. Anyone familiar with this theology will know how extensive, controversial and critical were the discussions in the 1930s, 1940s and 1950s of the definitions of the ends of marriage. In 1944 the Holy Office formulated the following question:

Can we admit the opinion of some recent writers who either deny that the primary end of marriage is the generation and bringing up of children or else teach that the secondary ends are not essentially subordinate to the primary end, but are in fact equally primary and independent? The answer given to this question is 'NO'.

Some twenty years later the Second Vatican Council not only abolished the usage of the terms 'primary and secondary ends', but had this to say, in direct contradiction to the answer of the Holy Office:

> Hence, while not making the other purposes of matrimony of less account, the true practice of conjugal love, and the whole meaning of the family life which results from it, have this aim: that the couple be ready with stout hearts to co-operate with the love of the Creator and the Saviour, who through them will enlarge and enrich His own family day by day.

In this statement the church places the personal and procreative elements on an equal footing.

I mention all this not to indulge in any special plea which shows the church to be fallible. I rejoice in the capacity of the church to examine the truth, formulate and teach it. I also agonise when that same church finds itself in isolation from the rest of the Christian community and from the overwhelming majority of its own people. Then, far from its teaching being prophetic, it becomes a danger to its task of revealing Christ to the world. It is no secret that one of the most urgent problems facing the church in Europe today is that survey after survey show that the majority of people believe in God but have withdrawn from the institution of the church. This withdrawal is a complex phenomenon but part of the problem is the inability of the church to speak accurately to man's contemporary experience. In sexual matters the church is not trusted. The constant answer to this aloofness is that the church possesses eternal truths which cannot be adapted to the popular whims of the day. This is perfectly true, but in matters of morals its teaching is based on a combination of scripture and natural law and, as discussed in the section on homosexuality (p. 18), the veracity of this teaching does not depend on mere repetition, however loud and authoritative, but on the humble and constant search of the meaning of the scriptures and the upholding of natural law. This requires a much greater co-operation between clergy and lay people than has been the habit in recent centuries.

The teaching of the Catholic Church on contraception is based on the conviction mentioned previously, that the sexual act has two meanings, a unitive and a procreative one, which must not be separated. In contraception there is a distortion of the 'total' donation of the husband and wife to each other.

To uphold this teaching it has to be shown unequivocally that there is a clear indication that the sexual act has two meanings, the unitive and the procreative, which must never be separated. This teaching is not drawn from the scriptures, as is that of fornication and adultery. I mention this, not to disparage the contribution of natural law to human thinking and the formulation of morality, but to make the point that our understanding of natural law is constantly developing as our knowledge of human nature unfolds. It is essential to moral thinking, based on natural law, that it changes as authentic insights about human nature make changes necessary.

One of the reasons why the teaching on contraception is so important to some Catholics is because of its continuity from the earliest days of Christianity. This is not the place to go into details but it has to be admitted that the goodness of coitus was seriously questioned in the early centuries of the church, although never repudiated. Against this hostile background procreation became a powerful and justifying element for its existence. Indeed a history of Christianity's attitude to sexual intercourse is intimately linked with the subordination of the personal loving meaning of coitus to the procreative one, which for a long time was its main justification. Thus when the church considers the subject of contraception, there is a long history in favour of the procreative potential and a relatively short and limited understanding of its unitive meaning. Since the married faithful, who are the principal agents of the meaning of coitus, have not played a crucial role in formulating the teaching, it is not surprising that their insights have not seriously contributed to it.

At its crudest, this teaching requires that every act of sexual intercourse should allow the unfettered deposition of semen in the vagina with no interference to the procreative potential of the fusion of sperm and ovum. At this level it is pure biology and must be assessed as such. Such a view is a throw-back to the ignorance of sexual physiology when the sperm was considered to be the agent of fertilisation. The discovery of the essential need of the ovum is of recent origin. If we look at God's design we find that women ovulate once a month, the ovum is capable of fertilisation on average for up to twenty-four hours and so the possibility of procreation is confined to an extremely limited period in each month. There is thus overwhelming evidence that the design of nature is not one that lends itself to find a procreative and unitive meaning in each and every sexual act.

A little more sophisticated argument indicates that procreation ultimately has nothing to do with the intricacies of biology, but with the human intention of bringing new life into being and loving it. Life is precious, not because it follows the rules of biology, but because of the richness of love. Furthermore the human propensity to create covers the whole period of fertility of the woman; there is not one iota of evidence which demands blind adherence to physiology in every act of coitus. Couples decide to have children when they are in the best position to look after them and love them. There is no rhyme or reason why they should not control their fertility in the best possible way to facilitate their family formation.

So far I have suggested that there is no evidence of any design in nature that demands that every sexual act should be open to life and no reason why the available fertility should not be controlled. But the protagonists of the teaching would proclaim that I am missing the point. The teaching is based on personal donation. Those who use contraception reduce their 'total' self-giving by suppressing the biological dimension. They are saying to each other that they are closed to a powerful dimension of their being. And even if they mutually agree to this, they have no right to do so because they remove a God-given potential.

My answer is that it is nowhere clear, as mentioned above, that the procreative potential has to be interpreted in every sexual act as against the fertility of the whole duration of marriage. The use of the infertile period closes the whole range of fertility of the couple. But the argument goes on that the use of the infertile period does not withhold the procreative potential, it chooses the natural periods of infertility. What it does, however, is far more serious, namely to withhold the persons of the spouses from each other.

Returning to the issue of personal donation of the spouses, the teaching on contraception argues that the frustration of the possible union between sperm and ovum is a vital distortion of the act: but this is a claim that is not recognised by every couple. Spouses know that their married love lies in the integrity of their relationship and this authenticity is to be found in their love. This love is directed first and foremost to the maintenance of their bond, that is, in the unity dimension of their relationship. If any one characteristic is appreciated as essential, it is the availability, in every act of intercourse, of the capacity to reinforce their bond. Men and women experience intercourse as a personal encounter of love in which the human characteristics, not the biological, are the supreme values. What matters to them primarily is the wellbeing of their spouse, not their fertility. Provided they are capable of having children, their mutual fertility is of no consequence to them. Indeed given that they are fertile and have had their children, the continuing presence of fertility is of little value except, after the possible death of one spouse, its use in another relationship.

This order of values between the procreative and the unitive is not appreciated by the teaching, which places them on an essentially equal basis. This is not how couples experience intercourse. For them, what is inherently needed in every act is the unitive potential described in this book as personal and sexual affirmation, reconciliation, hope, trust and

103

thanksgiving. The creative potential has a strictly limited application. Proponents of the teaching insist that the removal of this possibility will have dire personal and psychological consequences and point to the use of contraception before and outside marriage. My reply is that what is being discussed is contraception within marriage. In any case, sexual intercourse before and outside marriage has always been a temptation even before the advent of modern contraception. The other point made is that the non-availability of procreation has some dire psychological consequences. The suggestions for potential damage are numerous and varied but there is no convincing evidence for any. In particular, the one that is offered on behalf of marital breakdown, namely that those who divorce are more prone to use contraceptives, is a reason that has no serious social or psychological support. It is suggested above all that contraceptive intercourse dehumanises the couple because it removes the procreative potential. This is a theoretical supposition that has no evidence to support it. One has to remind the protagonists of these dangers that contraception has been around for a long time and, if discernible dangers to couples and society clearly existed, there would be irrefutable evidence, as there is in the case of marital breakdown.

In my writings I have suggested that, while I cannot follow the strict teaching on contraception, I can see that some contraceptives deter from the integrity of the sexual act, as for example in the case of the condom.

Finally the point is made that the use of the infertile period is a time of mutual sacrifice which is beneficial to the couple. The answer here is that married couples exercise a great deal of self-control at times of illness and non-availability for a variety of reasons. In my view the richness of coitus is such that there have to be excellent reasons for limiting its use.

For these and many other reasons I cannot in conscience follow this particular teaching, and in this respect, I have urged the church to reconsider it. The simplest way to do that is to ask the hierarchies of the world to test the opinion of their flock. This is one teaching that has been given but not received and, if authentic teaching has any meaning, it must express the life of the community of the faithful. The magisterium without the people of God is incomplete. While its teaching can never be based on popular consent, what it teaches must reflect the truth of the behaviour it describes. This truth cannot be based on theoretical abstracts but must be verified by human experience. In sexual matters it should reflect the wisdom of the married who are in a very much better position to test its accuracy. While I do not subscribe to the view that celibates are not capable of evaluating married truths, I am deeply concerned when the formulation of sexual ethics ignores the persistent and clear voice of the married. Is it likely that the grace of God, the discernment of the Holy Spirit, has deserted in substantial numbers the married whose sacrament makes them the most accurate interpreters of the meaning of sexual love?

One final point. The teaching on contraception, based on natural law, is meant to be clearly self-evident. Men and women abide by the rules. Why has so much of humanity become blind over contraception? Is it likely that, in this instance alone, there is widespread hardness of heart or clouding of the intellect? When so many of its own children and so much of the rest of the world are dissenting, is it surprising that there is such a large-scale ignoring of this teaching and would it not be more appropriate to think afresh? After all, no harm will be done to take the faithful into its confidence and ultimately express a view that reflects the whole Christian community. There is no point in describing the church as a KOINONIA and then to treat it as if it did not exist.

9

The Relationship between Coitus and Children

It has been argued that, increasingly in western society and gradually throughout the world, sexual intercourse in marriage will become the means of promoting the life of the couple and, on rare occasions, leading to new life. Whether contraception or the infertile period is used, the age-long link between coitus and procreation is being severed. For Christianity, which has relied so much on this link for its moral theology, the separation has produced severe problems. In this chapter I shall examine the link between coitus and children, no longer seen primarily in biological terms.

Size of the Family

A real distinction needs to be made between the morality of contraception and a contraceptive mentality. If the latter term is meant to explain the diminishing size of the contemporary family, this reduction needs a much more complex examination than the arrival of widespread contraception.

The diminution of family size is linked with such matters as standards of living, women's emancipation and a radical shift of appreciating quality rather than quantity in the number of children. There is little doubt that standards of living have risen considerably in the western 30 to 40 per cent of the world. While this elevation is pointing clearly to the injustices in other parts of the world and runs the risk of making western societies selfish and materialistic, there is little doubt that better standards of housing, health, nutrition, clothing and education are highly desirable objectives. What is urgently needed is to ensure that these standards can be achieved in the rest of the world. It is absolutely clear that the cost of raising children with contemporary western standards is high, and one of the contributing factors towards the diminution of family size is this cost. One way of meeting this expense is through the wife working, which reduces her availability as a mother.

Another factor contributing towards the curtailment of procreation is the emerging tension between parenting and work carried on outside the home. This is an issue of particular importance to women. There is little point in educating women if they are not allowed to realise their potential in work. This tension between work and the raising of children has been one of the dominating themes of western society in the post-war period. This is not the place to go into extensive detail, but many women feel that the predominantly male world of the church has not appreciated their dilemma. One of the answers to emerge is the conviction that parenting is not the sole preoccupation of women and that fathers have to share in the task. The progress towards combined responsibility of parenting has made some advances, but at the time of writing it is still primarily women who shoulder the triple responsibility of parenting, work and looking after the home.

This combination of factors has undoubtedly contributed to the diminishing family size. It has nothing to do with a contraceptive mentality. Rather it reflects an increasing awareness of human dignity in its various forms.

Another factor, already mentioned, which is playing a crucial role in the small sized family, is the increasing understanding of the needs of children. Their social and educational needs have to be supplemented by provision for their emotional growth, requiring awareness, sensitivity, empathy and love, as expressed through feelings, and an accurate understanding of the young person's developing psychology. Necessary to this is, above all, availability and time. Children can be serviced in their physical and intellectual needs but need a good deal of parental availability to meet their social and emotional needs. The growing awareness of these

107

requirements has led society in the last twenty-five years to become far more sensitive to the abuse of children, both physically and sexually.

So the reduction of family size is no indication of a contraceptive mentality, selfishness or indifference to children but of a concomitant of the complex factors existing in the West today. The single most important contribution to the prevailing and continuing concern for children is the immense attention paid to infertility, and the enormous sacrifices made by women to overcome this difficulty in order to become pregnant.

The ultimate reason for reducing fertility concerns the size of the world's population in relation to its resources. There are those who deny that there is any shortage of food for the requirements of the world population. This is opposed by the protagonists of the view that resources are limited and populations have to be contained. Whatever the ultimate truth of these contentions, the idea of a shrinking food availability, and hunger and poverty, have undoubtedly contributed to policies of the reduction of family size.

Parental Love

What has been lost in the link between coitus and procreation has been compensated by the growing psychological awareness that what children need above all is parental love, realised through marital stability. Study after study of children's lives show that what offspring require is the continuing, reliable and predictable love of their parents.

This love between husband and wife becomes their offspring's tuition in the meaning of love. The child sees in his parents the complementarity of the sexes, learns from them how to be a man or woman, how to give and receive, relate, fight and be reconciled, be available, make sacrifices, be generous, caring and forgiving; in brief to be a loving person. In order for all this to happen, parents have to remain in relationship with each other. The maintenance of this

108

parental bond is strongly influenced by regular and satisfactory coitus.

Thus the principal role of sexual intercourse within marriage in contemporary western society is the maintenance of the parental bond through which the child survives and develops. In saying this, contemporary Christians need to be reminded that the old definition of the purpose of marriage was divided into two parts. The primary end of marriage was the generation and upbringing of children, and secondarily the mutual help of spouses and the allaying of concupiscence.

These ends of marriage are no longer part of the teaching of the Roman Catholic Church. The Second Vatican Council dropped this formulation and talked of the family as a 'community of love' and an intimate partnership of 'life and love'. These words emphasise love. But the old definitions contained the seeds of truth. Children needed more than biology for their procreation, they required education. Similarly the allaying of concupiscence required more than the satisfaction of an instinct. The mutual help of the spouses was clearly appreciated.

What is happening today is that we have come to recognise that the emphasis on the biological and instinctual origins of sexuality is not the most appropriate way of interpreting its human dimensions. What *is* appropriate is to unite the two and to see them serving the whole family, through the reinforcement of the bond of the parents.

Thus the principal role of sexual intercourse is not the biology of procreation, essential though that is, but the maintenance of the parental love on which the life of the child ultimately depends for its development.

Preciousness of Children

The attitude of society towards children in the last twenty-five years can be summed up in the concept that parental generosity is not to be found in numbers, but in their care and attitude towards them. Children remain as precious as ever but they no longer constitute the predominant reason for marriage. Increasingly a balance is being struck between the realisation of the spouses' potential as persons and the care of their children. This division of interests has been interpreted as a withdrawal of concern for children. This is not the case. Children continue to hold the attention of parents, but there is an increasing realisation by spouses that they have a life of their own before the children arrive, and a protracted one after they depart. There is not the slightest evidence that society is being hostile to childbearing but a great deal that marital life is a sharing of personal and procreative goals. Children continue to receive appropriate attention but it is increasingly realised that their development requires the nurturing of the life of the parents and, for this, sexual intercourse is essential.

10

Sex and Marital Stability

The marital stability required by children is a complex phenomenon. Many books have been written on the subject and this chapter can only briefly review the topic and, in particular, the role played by sexual intercourse in the maintenance of this stability.

Life Cycle and Stability

Marital breakdown has been examined over the whole life cycle of marriage. What has emerged in many studies is that there are two peaks in divorce. These are in the first five years of marriage, and later on after the children have grown up and left home, that is, some twenty to thirty years after the beginning of marriage. It should be noted that the marriages which break up later in life are a new phenomenon historically, associated with the increased longevity of spouses. In between these two peaks there is a continuous incidence of divorce. In fact the current expectation of divorce in Britain is of the order of one in three marriages, and in the USA the figure is of the order of 40 per cent.

The available information suggests that the breakdown in the early years is indicative of the failure of the couple to establish a minimum conjugal relationship. When this occurs after many years of marriage it suggests a gradual alienation over time, which reveals itself after the children have left. What is common right through is that the survival of marriage depends on the couple meeting each other's social, emotional, sexual, intellectual and spiritual minimum needs, which vary over time.

In order to understand marital breakdown it is necessary to comprehend what these needs are for every married couple. No one has managed to achieve this yet, but the social sciences are beginning to point the way to a greater general understanding of what couples need. Detailed accounts of this are to be found in my two books, *Marriage, Faith and Love* and *Introduction to Marital Problems*. Here I am highlighting some of the points made in these books.

Marriage as a Relationship

Traditionally marriage was seen as a contract between a man and a woman which implied permanency, faithfulness and children. Civil divorce was granted when spouses offended against this contract, through desertion, adultery or cruelty. As already indicated, the divorce laws changed in the 1960s and so did the theology of marriage in the Christian community, particularly in the Second Vatican Council. Both theology and law made a significant shift in understanding marriage as a relationship, whose stability depended on the continuity of its viability. The civil law made 'irretrievable breakdown of marriage' the sole ground for petitioning for divorce. The ecclesiastical courts interpret relationship indirectly, so when marriages fail their validity is assessed on the grounds whether the couple lacked due discretion regarding the essential matrimonial rights and obligations or, because of psychological reasons, they were unable to assume the essential obligations of marriage. In both instances the couple are incapable of maintaining a viable relationship. This shift from contract to relationship is a fundamental change in contemporary marriage, and demands a better understanding of what couples need from one another.

Needs of Couples

The needs of couples are many and complex. There are social, emotional, sexual, intellectual and spiritual requirements. At

112

the social level couples need a house and material resources to run it. Both these provisions are the responsibility of society. Within the house the couple have to relate intellectually, that is, communicate, share opinions and attitudes and reconcile their differences. Spiritually, they may have a common faith and values, and once again they have to make sense of different outlooks.

However the most important needs in contemporary marriage are those which express their affection and sexual love for each other. How has affectivity come to have such a tremendous importance in the West? The realisation of many material objectives, such as food, shelter and work, has meant that human beings are striving for fulfilment at a deeper layer of their being. Their priorities are no longer to overcome starvation, disease and lack of housing. In the presence of these they concentrate on really knowing each other through affection and sexuality. For Christians whose ultimate goal is to be as perfect as their heavenly Father who is love, this movement towards affectivity is to be welcomed. It presents enormous challenges and is also responsible for the break-down of many marriages. But it is a goal utterly compatible with Christian revelation. The challenge is to understand how affectivity is interpreted by couples. Here, a combination of clinical and psychological experiences has led me to suggest that men and women yearn for three things in which affection is vital. They long for sustaining, for healing and for growth.

Sustaining

All of us are the product of our childhood. It is in these first fifteen to twenty years of our life that we have learnt the meaning of being sustained and in this sustaining, love played a prominent part. Thus we associate intimacy with love. The first intimate relationship is between parents and ourselves and the second is often between husband and wife. In marriage social and material sustaining is essential but, if these are available, then the focus shifts to the emotions.

Emotional sustaining is first experienced in accurate and

113

sensitive communication. Deep inside all of us lies the longing to be understood with the same accuracy as our parents did. Men and women want to know and be known as fully as possible, but in order for this to happen effective communication is necessary. This requires that the couple find time to talk to one another. Such conversation needs more than an exchange of words. The couple need to recognise the feelings and moods of each other. Sustaining means being listened to, understood and responded to accurately. This accuracy demands much more than rational understanding. It needs the empathy of having our hopes ascertained and the signals of pain, misery, anxiety, fear, hope or joy received and responded to. If this emotional sustaining is not achieved then couples relate socially, intellectually and sexually and yet still feel lonely, as their inner world is not touched.

These emotional needs are particularly in evidence at times of stress. When spouses are in distress because they are ill, harassed, bereaved or depressed, that is the time when they require comfort, support and understanding. A combination of sensitive awareness, coupled with tender response, is what couples expect from each other.

Such emotional depth is not easily achieved. In general women are more inclined to be emotionally aware, to communicate better and to be more affectionately available than men, although there are many exceptions to this generalisation. Whatever their individual resources, spouses need to learn about each other's requirements and deepen their ability for mutual understanding.

Healing

In the depths of this emotional exchange, couples reveal to each other their wounds. These may be social, physical or emotional. It is the emotional ones that stand out, and they originate in two ways. The first is through the genetic constitution. Nowadays we recognise that genes contribute to our moods of anxiety and depression, our tendency to be irritable

114

and aggressive, despondent or optimistic, rigid or flexible. The second source of our wounding is our upbringing.

Even the most perfect set of parents can leave a trail of distress behind. Psychiatrists see the extreme forms of emotional deprivation, hurt, neglect or abuse in adults. But all of us are likely to have feelings of lack of confidence or shyness, feeling unlovable or unwanted, sensitive or easily criticised. In the depths of intimacy that couples experience, these feelings which quickly reach the surface are a prominent feature of the relationship.

A loving union can foster healing. Thus a wife or husband who is emotionally deprived, who longs for affection and approval, can have as their partner someone who is blessed with a capacity to be loving and affirming. Over many years the wounded individual receives continuous affection and acceptance which helps them to overcome their sense of being unlovable.

It is usual for couples to complement each other. Thus when one partner is lacking in confidence the other is reassuring; when one is diffident the other is confident; introversion is matched by extroversion, and so on. This healing takes time and it needs the continuity of the marriage for it to be effective. In all probability marriage is the single most important source of healing in society, but for this to take place an emotional dialogue is necessary.

Growth

Couples who remain married over fifty years do not stay the same throughout all this period. They change. Socially one or both spouses may rise or drop in their socioeconomic standing. Success at work means a rise in social status; a family acquires new friends and leads a different style of life. Illness, alcoholism, unemployment are often associated with a drop in social position. Both elevation and diminution in social standing need adjustment which, if not realised, means that couples become alienated and go their separate ways.

This alienation is also in evidence intellectually as couples

115

change in their attitudes, opinions and values. They have to learn to adjust to each other. This means that they need to respect views they no longer share.

In the course of mutual growth spouses form a relationship in which there is a balance of individuality and mutuality; of independence and dependence; of privacy and unity; separateness and oneness. But in this delicately poised relationship the attachment of love remains. This is a love that continues to contribute vitally to each other's life.

One expression of this love is the deep understanding of each other which allows the unconscious, unrealised potential of the individual to be facilitated by the partner. A spouse may be unsure, confused, hesitant about what they want to do or lacking in confidence to complete a particular venture. The partner may help them to clarify or to evaluate their objectives. Spouses may want to try new recipes, jobs, decorate, write books, and are not sure of their intentions or the ability to start and formulate their projects. They need their spouse's love, which facilitates in the same way that a midwife does a pregnancy.

This love is also seen in the exchange of personal affection. Too often spouses and friends believe the best way to stimulate a loving response is to remind their partner unceasingly of all their shortcomings. They think the best way to love is by mobilising the guilt, and therefore the reform, of their spouse. In fact most of us know only too well what is wrong with us. What we need is encouragement and affirmation to overcome our difficulties. Couples gradually learn to suppress their criticism and instead increase the frequency of praise and acclamation. In this way love is deepened.

Sexual Intercourse

It has already been shown that sexual intercourse has a wide range of personal meaning which makes it particularly apt to be expressed in the continuous relationship we call marriage.

But in this chapter we see that the stability of marriage depends on the ability of the couple to meet their mutual social, emotional, physical, intellectual and spiritual needs. There is an order of priority and, as the material and social requirements are met, it is the inner world of emotions that become paramount, experienced through sustaining, healing and growth. A great deal of contemporary marital breakdown is an expression of the lack of these three key areas.

Sexual intercourse plays a prominent part in fulfilling these three characteristics. Once the couple are married they begin a journey which is unique to them. They share a history which is inimitable. Sexual intercourse plays a vital part in this exchange and is far more than an instinctual or procreative energy. It is life-giving. It forms the background against which the couple get to know each other. In the Old Testament the word for coitus is to 'know', and this is an excellent psychological understanding of the contribution of sexual intercourse.

Every time the couple make love the consummation of pleasure and joy gives them strength to sustain each other. Their physical intimacy reinforces their intellectual and emotional knowledge of each other. Even if they have some distance to cover in comprehending one another, successful intercourse offers a taste of complete awareness of their feelings and their bodies. The physical and emotional dimensions of coitus become the channels of further interpersonal communication, and through intercourse they give to each other a message of rich intention. They are determined to make their bodily and emotional experiences the basis for further exploration of mutual understanding. Successful coitus creates an atmosphere through which they are prepared to listen afresh, be open to new nuances and feel a desire to comprehend and reduce mutual differences.

Sexual intercourse has a special place in healing. It is the supreme gesture of unconditional acceptance of each other. The hurt, deficient, limited partner is received repeatedly without reservation. For each hurt received in childhood, there is now loving acceptance. The effort to overcome limitations now receives affirmation. The pain caused by the spouse is forgiven in the depths of the climax. Sexual

117

intercourse breaks down barriers of isolation, deprivation, self-rejection, for at the moment of the orgasm all pain is removed.

Coitus makes a significant contribution to the balance of unity and diversity of marital life. It is an act which by its very nature brings together two separate people and reduces them into one. In sexual intercourse the tension between separateness and togetherness is overcome, as the couple become one without losing their separate identities.

Thus sexual intercourse in marriage is always taking place in the context of an ongoing relationship and now has a dynamism which can never be realised in the context of casual and transient relationships. It is an act that signifies and realises the complete mutual donation of the partners. Thus intercourse with a third party (discussed in Chapters 3 and 7) becomes a violation of this exclusive exchange of love.

11

Adultery

Whatever the tolerance that may have been shown in the last
quarter of a century to premarital coitus or cohabitation,
survey after survey show that western society holds fidelity in
high esteem and condemns adultery. Despite this disapproval
extramarital sexual activity continues; but, just as in the case
of premarital intercourse so now in the case of adultery, it is
essential to try to understand different categories of adulterous
behaviour.

It is important to distinguish between casual adultery that
does not threaten the marital relationship, which remains
intact, and the situation in which the marriage is in serious
difficulties and the extramarital relationship is a symptom of
a deteriorating conjugal situation.

Casual Adultery

In the category of casual adultery will be found the sexual
activity of husbands and wives who are temporarily away
from each other and have sex with a perfect stranger. The
reason for this may be a deep sense of loneliness or anxiety
at being alone. If they are absent for long periods there
may be a physical need. Whatever the reason, these casual
exchanges do not threaten the stability of the marriage but
they may be discovered by catching a venereal infection and
transmitting it to the spouse. Clearly the advent of AIDS has
infinitely more serious consequences than those prevailing in
the past.

In the same category will be found the sexual contact of

the husband at times of the wife's pregnancy, illness or non-availability for a variety of reasons. Again, either spouse may have sex under the influence of drink; or when they are cross with each other they may have extramarital sex as an expression of revenge. In a similar vein are extramarital affairs affecting spouses who are changing and want to understand themselves better: having an affair helps them to feel more lovable or sexually acceptable but they have no intention of breaking their marriage.

In this category of adulterous relationships are often to be found bisexual men who, while wishing to remain faithful to their wives, have homosexual liaisons. This is not uncommon and is particularly risky with AIDS in mind.

Serious Adultery

Finally a whole host of extramarital relationships occur as the direct result of the deteriorating relationship of the marriage. This is the most serious form of adultery. Having given up any hope of improving the marriage, spouses have affairs with third parties which may become the alternative relationship in their life.

Response to Adultery

In the Judaeo-Christian tradition the stability of the marriage carries the supreme value, and forgiveness and reconciliation are the suggested responses to extramarital intercourse. Beyond forgiveness, it is essential for spouses to understand why their partner has needed to resort to sex outside the marriage. The difference between casual and meaningful adultery is fundamental.

That is not to say that the pain and sense of betrayal is any less, whatever the kind of adultery. Spouses understandably feel that through extramarital sex their partner is rejecting them. This rejection is often considered to be personal and what suffers most is the trust the couple have in each other. While they can forgive their partner, they find it much harder to forget and to build trust afresh.

But in forgiving, the betrayed spouse has to consider their own contribution to the act of adultery. Have they played a part in any way? Have they provided their partner with enough affection and/or sexual intercourse? It is essential to go beyond forgiveness to a mutual understanding of the reasons that led to the adultery.

AIDS and Adultery

It has already been pointed out that bisexual men may become infected with the AIDS virus and transmit this to their wives. The advent of AIDS poses a new need for marital fidelity. In the depths of the Judaeo-Christian tradition of fidelity there is an understanding that the exclusive relationship between husband and wife is a symbol of the covenant in the Old Testament between Yahweh and Israel and in the New Testament between Christ and the church.

Thus faithfulness is much more than a need not to infect one's spouse. It is an expression of that total love between spouses which signifies their sense of unity and oneness.

This unity of the couple will not be safeguarded by the husband wearing a condom. An awareness of the danger of infection should be pointing the way to understanding the multiple reasons for adulterous behaviour. It is not enough to preach fidelity and it is certainly not in the least relevant to make procreation an essential expression of coitus in order to help couples avoid adultery.

What is far more important is to try to understand the human personality and the nature of relationships. In this respect I hope fervently that the dreadful disease of AIDS will encourage all the churches to rethink their priorities with regard to contemporary marriage and consider it essential to allocate money and resources as an urgent matter to understanding the central role of coitus in marital stability.

12

The Importance of Marital Stability

The central theme that runs through this book is that human sexuality is a uniquely powerful force whose purpose is to attract men and women into pairing, and subsequently to maintaining this bond which we call marriage. In this scheme marital stability and the family assume supreme values. I want to describe briefly why marital stability is so important and to reiterate a main concern of mine that Christianity has not given marital permanency the significance it deserves.

Despite Pope John Paul II's statement in Familiaris Consortio, 'To bear witness to the inestimable value of the indissolubility and fidelity of marriage is one of the most precious and most urgent tasks of Christian couples in our time', the Roman Catholic Church has been preoccupied during the last twenty years, a time of unprecedented rise of divorce, with contraception, an issue which, as mentioned previously, pales into insignificance compared with marital breakdown.

General Effect

In agreeing to marry, a man and woman feel so much in love with one another that they want to spend the rest of their life together. Marital breakdown can be bitter and traumatic or less acrimonious or even apathetic. Whatever the attitude of the couple at the time of the dissolution, what is inevitable is an erosion in the conviction and trust that love is possible. A certain amount of cynicism always accompanies divorce. It is true that the need for pairing is so powerful that a very high percentage of divorcees remarry and that second marriages can be successful. In fact however in Britain second marriages are one and a half to twice as likely as first marriages to end in divorce. But however much wiser couples may be after experiencing one divorce, the fact is that subsequent relationships do not as a rule have the clarity and conviction of motivation of the first relationship. Second and third marriages are forged much more on a combination of reality and the possible than on the richness of sacrificial first love which engages the deepest elements of the personality. Given human frailty second marriages will always be a necessity when the first relationship is cut short by death or divorce. But what most couples wish is the fullest realisation of their first hopes of love.

In addition to the general disappointment of a failed marriage, couples who experience the end of one relationship are not likely to be so open and trusting the second time. Their object is often to protect themselves from being hurt again so there is a tendency to play safe. Generosity can be replaced by prudence. Instead of living subsequent relationships at the extreme end of openness, the aim is often to ensure that nothing happens to them and survival may become the predominant theme. No one can blame couples participating in second marriages in their desire to be cautious. But all this suggests how important it is to prepare and support first marriages.

Impact of Marital Breakdown on Spouses

Marriage is a specific attachment of a man to a woman and when that bond is threatened the spouses experience anger, anxiety, depression and all its consequences.

The first awareness that something is seriously wrong in a relationship is realised when either partner feels that a fundamental need is not being met. The requirement may be social, emotional or sexual. After persistent efforts to convince their spouse are met with failure, what follows is anger. This anger may be ventilated or suppressed. When it is suppressed it leads to sulking, withdrawal and a general misery. Psychiatrists recognise that suppressed anger leads to frustration, irritation and depression and these exist in plenty in relationships which are in discord. This state of tension may also produce physical manifestations of tiredness, insomnia and inability to function effectively.

The next stage of marital difficulties is experienced after the failure of anger and quarrels to produce the desired effect and change behaviour. Now there is increasing anxiety about the potential loss of the spouse. We become agitated at the threat of losing someone who matters to us and to whom we have a deep attachment. Couples expecting to lose their spouse are in a constant state of anxiety, which is manifested in overt worry and physical manifestations of distress.

The final stage is reached when the spouse departs. Now the prevailing mood is that of sadness. This sadness is the consequence of the severance of the bond and the subsequent loss of someone who has been significant in our life. The sadness may turn into an overt depression characterised by pronounced misery, loss of energy, insomnia, loss of appetite, weight loss, lack of concentration, poor memory and a general inability to function.

These stresses, present in various stages of persistent and severe marital difficulties, can lead the person to turn to excessive smoking or alcohol, the consequences of the latter being particularly damaging. But the risk that exists above all is that of suicidal attempt or suicide itself. Every study of parasuicide, as suicidal attempt has come to be called, shows that marital difficulties are a prominent feature preceding the attempt to take one's own life.

A combination of all these manifestations explains why marital conflict is such a common contributor to ill health and is associated with frequent visits to the doctor.

After marital breakdown takes place, the couples separate and live lonely lives. Research evidence shows that during the period after separation and before a new and meaningful relationship has been established, the risk of suicide is very high indeed.

124

Independently of the risk of suicide, many divorces are associated with the presence of children under the age of sixteen. The one-parent family has multiplied in society as divorce has increased.

While some fathers look after their children, the vast majority of young children live with their mother and there is an army of one-parent families formed by women and their children; in Britain the number is of the order of a million. These men and women have been repeatedly shown to constitute one of the most deprived sections of the community. They are deprived economically in the sense that not all of them find it easy to work when they are caring for their young children. They are handicapped socially in that they are often isolated, excluded from social functions aimed at couples, and find it difficult to go out and meet people. They are also emotionally deprived, often lacking the reassurance and comfort of an intimate relationship, even if they are supported by friends and relatives.

Thus marital breakdown has a profound and manifold adverse impact on spouses, ranging from physical and psychological manifestations to the persistent difficulties of the one-parent status. In the current spate of divorce, involving some 350,000 men and women annually in the United Kingdom, this is accumulatively one of the most serious contributors to social pathology in our society.

Impact on Children

At the start of the divorce wave in the sixties and early seventies there was a general belief that divorce did not cause much damage to children. But recent studies suggest the opposite. In fact the studies of the 1980s have shown increasingly that few children escape unscathed. The remarks that follow are taken from numerous published papers and reflect only the major findings.

One major American study found that pre-school children were frightened and tended to blame themselves. They could not understand what was happening, divorce at this age being

SEXUAL INTEGRITY: THE ANSWER TO AIDS

particularly traumatic. Young school children express feelings of sadness, abandonment and rejection. They think their mother sends father away and wish desperately to reconcile their parents. Older school children can realise that divorce is a parental affair but are shocked by the behaviour. They feel angry, lonely and rejected. Adolescents are very upset and express strong feelings of anger, misery, shame and embarrassment.

The disturbance of mood can be accompanied by misconduct at school and at home and a regression to earlier behaviour of bed-wetting, clinging, demands for affection and general distress. Sometimes the behaviour is antisocial and can be associated with stealing, destroying objects, shouting and disobedience. All this can last up to two years and sometimes much longer, depending on the relationship the children establish with their separated parents. A British study has shown that children of divorced or separated parents were much more likely than other children to have lower educational qualifications by the age of twenty-six. By comparison, parental death has little impact on the child's later educational achievements.

The impact of divorce on children is not exhausted in the adverse consequences in childhood. Children whose parents were divorced or separated before they were five years old were more likely to commit serious crimes in early adult life and/or more commonly need inpatient psychiatric care in hospital. Marital breakdown is associated in children with a higher rate of mood disorders in later adolescence or adulthood.

There are also associations between marital breakdown and the sexual behaviour of the children involved. Several studies suggest that teenage pregnancies and illegitimate births are more frequent for girls whose parents separated in childhood. It is likely that children, bruised emotionally by parental discord, will lack the affection they need and may revert to early and indiscriminate sexual behaviour to compensate for this deprivation. There is evidence that girls whose parents

126

separated when they were very young tend to resort to earlier heterosexual behaviour.

Finally and most serious of all, both in the United States and in Britain, studies have shown that for children from broken homes a higher proportion of their own marriages break down than for those from intact homes. Thus a vicious circle is established whereby the instability of the parents' marriage predisposes the children to a similar pattern.

Moral Implications

This brief excursion into the damaging effect of marital breakdown is important for two reasons. First the size and consequences of divorce make me repeat here what I have already said elsewhere, that this is one of, if not the most serious of social and moral problems of our day. It is essential for the Christian community to appreciate this and combat it by directing resources for research and pastoral energy at preventive measures.

Secondly marital breakdown is a paradigm for assessing moral issues. Despite the existence of divorce in the Old Testament, the whole emphasis of the Old and the New Testament is clearly against it and, in the case of divorce, we have a clear direction from Jesus himself. Tradition has maintained the ban against it and finally in our day the damaging consequences have been clearly shown. These three factors, revelation, tradition and overt consequences, have a powerful impact on men and women. Even if the law is flouted, there remains powerful belief in the ideal. In comparison the most disputed issue of our day in the Catholic Church, namely contraception, has only tradition to support it, which clearly is not enough.

13

Human Sexuality:
Secular Reality and Divine Mystery

Introduction

Human sexuality, as we have seen, combines attraction, pairing, the maintenance of a bond and procreation. Between them they form the foundation of family life and society. In many respects this energy is the cornerstone of our humanity and, as such, deserves a central place in Christian life. Unfortunately this has not been the case, not for the lack of revelation of its significance, but because throughout the Christian tradition its development has been poor in the extreme. In this chapter I shall examine in outline the scriptural, traditional and current moral position on the subject.

Secular Reality and Divine Mystery

Under the heading of secular reality and divine mystery I want to show that sexuality has been made sacred. In other words human beings and their sexuality reflect and point to the divine nature.

We see this at the very beginning of the Bible, in Genesis. In the first chapter we find God saying:

> 'Let us make man in our own image, in the likeness of ourselves, and let them be masters of the fish of the sea, the birds of heaven, the cattle, all the wild animals and all the creatures that creep along the ground.'

> God created man in the image of himself;

in the image of God he created him,
male and female he created them. (1:26–27)

and a little later on, the basic goodness of sexuality is
confirmed: 'God saw all he had made, and indeed it was very
good' (1:31).

This goodness is underlined in the poetry of the Song of
Songs. Here is the man appreciating the girl:

How beautiful you are, my beloved,
how beautiful you are!
Your eyes are doves,
behind your veil;
your hair is like a flock of goats
surging down Mount Gilead.
Your teeth, a flock of sheep to be shorn
when they come up from the washing.
Each one has its twin,
not one impaired with another.
Your lips are a scarlet thread
and your words enchanting.
Your cheeks, behind your veil,
are halves of pomegranate.
Your neck is the Tower of David
built on layers,
hung round with a thousand bucklers,
and each the shield of a hero.
Your two breasts are two fawns,
twins of a gazelle,
that feed among the lilies. (4:1–5)

This beautiful appraisal of feminine beauty is answered by
the woman:

My love is fresh and ruddy,
to be known among ten thousand.
His head is golden, purest gold,
his locks are palm fronds
and black as the ravens.

129

His eyes are like doves
beside the water-courses,
bathing themselves in milk,
perching on a fountain-rim.
His cheeks are beds of spices,
banks sweetly scented.
His lips are lilies,
distilling pure myrrh.
His hands are golden, rounded,
set with jewels of Tarshish.
His belly a block of ivory
covered with sapphires.
His legs are alabaster columns
set in sockets of pure gold.
His appearance is that of Lebanon,
unrivalled as the cedars.
His conversation is sweetness itself,
he is altogether lovable.
Such is my love, such is my friend,
O daughters of Jerusalem. (5:10–16)

There is little doubt that in this poem we are in the midst of one of the most powerful forces of mutual human attraction placed in mankind by the Creator for a purpose. What is it? The answer is to be found in Genesis.

The second narrative in Genesis describes how God found man's aloneness unsatisfactory: 'God said, "It is not right that the man should be alone. I shall make him a helper"' (2:18). I want to stress here that the key to understanding human sexuality is to be found in the concept of *relationship*. Although this is abundantly clear in the Judaeo-Christian tradition, the fact that it has not become the unequivocal interpretation of its meaning in Christian circles is one of the greatest weaknesses of that faith. But the scriptures leave no room for doubt. After the description of how woman was created out of man, the man proclaims:

This one at last is bone of my bones

130

and flesh of my flesh!
She is to be called Woman,
because she was taken from Man.

This is why a man leaves his father and mother and becomes attached to his wife, and they become one flesh.

Now, both of them were naked, the man and his wife, but they felt no shame before each other. (2:23–25)

This passage directs our attention to the fact that the essence of sexuality points to relationship between the sexes, whose ultimate consummation is the oneness of coitus. This in turn reflects the mystery of the Trinity where the three persons are constantly in a relationship of love, which makes them one, and yet they retain their separate identity, just as the couple do.

It is only when the couple form a relationship that revelation shows should be permanent, that procreation is possible. The priority is clearly on relationship first and procreation second, an order of events which the theology of Christianity has yet fully to comprehend. It is only within a loving relationship that procreation makes full sense because the child's primary need is to be loved. In loving the child, the parents are repeating the divine plan that God so loved the world that he created it and redeemed it. All revelation leads to love, not to biology. Procreation is a divine blessing, not an instinct shared with animals.

In the first account of creation the writer says: 'God blessed them, saying to them, "Be fruitful, multiply, fill the earth and subdue it" ' (Gen. 1:28). The world is undoubtedly made to be continued and coitus is the means of doing this. But this fruitfulness is not an acclamation of instinct but of love, for the loving components of sexual intercourse are its essential elements.

The concept that love is the inner reality of coitus is next expressed in the concept of covenant. The covenant between God and Israel, his chosen people, was a special relationship of love. It was a bond of absolute commitment and fidelity

131

on the part of God which elicited a response of obedience and love from his people. Whenever Israel failed to be faithful, God showed his constancy by repeated forgiveness and a continuous outpouring of love.

From the time of the prophet Hosea, one way of portraying this relationship was through marriage. This covenant marriage is also found in Jeremiah, Ezekiel and Isaiah. In all these prophets Israel's lack of fidelity is described in conjugal terms of the unfaithfulness of the wife who behaves like a 'harlot' or a 'whore'. The whole point of the imagery is God's desire to remain faithful, loving, forgiving; to preserve the relationship, now seen as a conjugal bond. Thus in Hosea we read:

> I shall betroth you to myself for ever,
> I shall betroth you in uprightness and justice,
> and faithful love and tenderness.
> Yes, I shall betroth you to myself in loyalty,
> and in the knowledge of Yahweh. (Hos. 2:21–22)

By using marriage as a symbol of the intimacy between God and Israel, these prophets revealed to us the nature of the marriage relationship, grounded on love. Thus human love, the secular reality of marriage, is taken up and becomes a reflection of the divine mystery of God's love, and at its heart lies commitment, permanency and unity.

These characteristics of love in marriage are taken up by St Paul in his letter to the Ephesians, where the relationship between the God of Israel and his people is now extended in the new covenant between Christ and the church. Once again marriage is used as a symbol of this love relationship:

> Husbands should love their wives, just as Christ loved the Church and sacrificed himself for her . . . In the same way, husbands must love their wives as they love their own bodies; for a man to love his wife is for him to love himself. A man never hates his own body, but he feeds it and looks after it; and that is the way Christ treats the Church, because we are parts of his Body. This is why a man leaves

132

his father and mother and becomes attached to his wife, and the two become one flesh. This mystery has great significance, but I am applying it to Christ and the Church. (Eph.5:25,28–32)

In these few passages we see a line of thought from the scriptures that sees human sexuality as something fundamentally good, a secular reality ordained for the attraction of the sexes, expressing love in the unity of the couple in marriage and being fruitful in children. Repeatedly this secular reality reflects the divine mystery of God himself, the mystery being shown in person, relationship and love, which ultimately finds expression in the divine dynamism of three persons constantly relating in love with each other in the Trinity.

Tradition

This richness of the secular reality in sexuality being taken up in the divine mystery is not, alas, continued in the Christian tradition. Rather, it finds itself surrounded, at worst by suspicion and hostility, and at best its integrity is preserved in marriage primarily when it serves as a procreative function. It is no exaggeration to say that, for most of the two thousand years of Christianity, the voice of the church welcomed sexuality principally as a channel for new life. Its inner world of rich meaning and the link with love were occasionally hinted at but never taken up in substance. There is no better book in print to record the fate of sexuality from the early centuries until recent times than J. T. Noonan's *Contraception*. The ascendancy of procreation over the relationship of the spouses, as far as the meaning of sexuality is concerned, remained in force in the Roman Catholic Church until the Second Vatican Council when the two were put on an equal footing. Nevertheless, it is abundantly clear from the scriptures and the experience of the couple that the human meaning of sexuality has as its primary significance the exploration of love, a human love which points the way to divine love.

How is it then that the Holy Spirit, while protecting the

church from seeing sex and procreation as evil – which was the view of Gnosticism – nevertheless failed to promote its unique meaning within the church?

There are several reasons for this. First the church has always been faced from the very beginning with the fact of the virgin birth of our Lord and, in paying the right attention to our Lady, had to emphasise virginity. Secondly the early church was influenced by Greek thought and, for a section of this, detachment from passion played an important part. Epicurus is said to have declared, 'Nobody was ever the better for the carnal act and man may be thankful if he was not definitely the worse.' Thirdly, while the early church was able to shake off the heresies of the Manicheans, their hostility towards sexuality left its mark. Fourthly, while both our Lord and St Paul had wonderful things to say about marriage, the fact remains that Jesus was a celibate and Paul had a predilection for that state. Our Lord, while totally approving of marriage, praised the single state dedicated to God. Fifthly some of the fathers of the early church were hostile to sexuality. In the light of our modern psychological understanding of the human personality we can see that one way of dealing with a sexual problem is by denying its value altogether. This undoubtedly played a part in some of the thought of the early fathers, especially in the case of Augustine who influenced the church so much on the subject of sexuality and marriage and who had such marked personal problems in sexual matters.

But, above all, there cannot be a rich theology of marital sex without a pre-eminence of marriage in the life of the church. By general agreement marriage has been the most neglected sacrament in the Roman Catholic Church. This is not surprising. For hundreds of years celibate clergy have been considered to be the predominant voice, and the laity hardly existed in their own right. A rich theology of sex or marriage needs the married to contribute to its spirituality. The laity and the married, who constitute 90 per cent of the church, assumed theological significance in the Roman Catholic Church only after the Second Vatican Council, and have yet to find their voice, and, indeed, the confidence to articulate their thoughts.

But, it will be argued, the Protestant tradition with its married clergy has also failed to make a distinctive contribution to the theology of sexuality. This is so, although a married clergy has undoubtedly contributed to an appreciation of contraception, which has been accepted.

I think in fairness to the whole Christian tradition it must be said that, given the social and psychological limitations of understanding that have prevailed for the major part of the church's history, the lack of theological progress in sexual matters is not surprising.

The important conclusion is to appreciate that, in this area of human thought and experience, Christian tradition is important, yet limited. This has tremendous implications for moral theology. In such matters as, for example, contraception and masturbation, moral conclusions have been drawn against a background of marked poverty of understanding sexuality. While I am at one with the mind of the church in wishing to emphasise the importance of tradition in assessing moral matters, it is important to stress that those who wish to formulate sexual morality in strict accordance with this tradition must recognise its limitations, and not be frightened by radical alterations to moral principles. I cannot emphasise too strongly this point which taxes conservative theologians to the extreme. How can the Spirit allow the church to teach error for so long, they say, if the teaching on contraception, for example *is* wrong? I can understand this anxiety. The fact is that God continuously reveals the richness of his creation as human beings unfold and realise its truths through the means he places in their hands. As far as contraception is concerned it is only now, when coitus is no longer needed primarily for procreational purposes and because infant mortality has been reduced substantially, that we can go beyond its creative meaning and see its fruitfulness in terms of the interpersonal love of the couple. The key to moral authenticity is to be found in the Judaeo-Christian tradition,

135

when the results which emerge are consistent with the revealed truths in the scriptures.

In the Christian tradition of sexuality, as I have frequently pointed out, the biology of coitus has been of primary significance. We now realise that it is the loving components of the act which are predominant and point the way to divine love. This understanding, largely due to contemporary psychological insights, is congruent with revelation.

Natural Law

A good deal of moral teaching on sexuality including contraception is not based on specific scriptural texts, for in addition to the scriptures, the Roman Catholic Church uses a theology based on natural law. In its natural law theology the church has considered it possible to reach moral conclusions through which all men and women can see the truth about human behaviour independently of revelation. In the words of the moral theologian Fr J. Mahoney 'The claim, and indeed the pride, of the Catholic tradition of natural law argumentation has been that moral principles can be established not just for believers but for all men and women simply by reflecting upon the reality of God's human creation as a source of moral enlightenment' (*Tablet*, 21 March 1987).

Augustine believed that God's eternal law was 'impressed' on his creatures. Aquinas examined this eternal law in the nature of the things God had created. In other words, by examining the nature of things man could reach God's intention of how they should be used and not abused. Aquinas discovered three fundamental dynamisms which had moral implications.

The first and most basic is the one we share with all created creatures, preservation: to resist destruction and continue in existence. Hence all activity that is concerned with killing is wrong, from which derives, for example, the morality of abortion and euthanasia.

The second principle, again shared with all creatures, is to ensure the survival of our species, which in this book I have described as the biology of procreation. From this principle all sexual behaviour could be organised; indeed, a great deal of traditional Roman Catholic sexual ethics depends on this concept. Certainly the teaching on contraception which specifies that every sexual act should be open to life is intimately related to this view.

The third principle applies to human beings alone and is a natural inclination, with two characteristics: our rationality, leading to the pursuit of truth; and life in community, with all the resulting moral implications of love.

No one can underestimate the value of natural law and the invaluable contributions that this concept, heavily influenced by the thought of Aquinas, has made to Catholic thought, to all Christianity and to society. As recently as the reign of Pope Pius XII, the Catholic Church placed an enormous importance on natural law as a basis for a just society and as the answer to medical ethics. But, although the advantages have been extensive, the arguments about what constitutes human nature have also multiplied, leading to many difficulties and problems.

The Second Vatican Council did not abrogate moral principles drawn from natural law but it emphasised, not human nature as such but the human person, as the fundamental source of morality. The dignity of the human person is central in the 'Pastoral Constitution on the Church in the Modern World' and the immensely important section on 'Marriage and the Family in the Modern World' is to be found in this constitution.

This shift of emphasis from nature to person has accelerated a process of renewal in moral theology, based on natural law, which had started before the council sat. This review, based on a personal morality, is common to all theologians who are attempting to formulate moral theology afresh. As can be expected there has been considerable disagreement on the conclusions to be drawn from the changes briefly outlined here. At least two schools of thought have emerged, one associated with Germain Grisez and the other called 'Consequentialism'. It would take us a long way from the theme of this book to digress any further on these two schools of thought, but as far as sexual ethics are concerned the former group agrees more with traditional teaching, while the latter takes different positions. In the context of this book it is worth noting that the position taken on contraception, for example, is shared by many moral theologians around the world.

As far as I am concerned, I would like to clarify that I believe profoundly in objective norms for sexual ethics which have to be interpreted on the basis of person, relationship and love, and of these three, love is the supreme criterion. My understanding of person and relationship is based on my own psychological insights, and on love in the conviction that it is the ultimate basis for Christian belief, since the nature of God, according to St John, is love.

It can be seen that the soundest moral formulations are those in which scriptures, tradition and natural law are clearly and unequivocally in agreement. Some sexual ethics, such as fornication, adultery and divorce, can be thus formulated and present fewer problems. The word 'fewer' is used advisedly because, even in the case of marriage, there are arguments about the scriptural sayings on divorce and, in the absence of scriptural teaching, the position on contraception has been very problematical. So what are we to do? The average Roman Catholic will say without hesitation that the answer is to follow the teaching of the church, which leads me to the concept of the magisterium.

Magisterium

The New Testament recognises two moral authorities. First there is the Johannine view that the believer receives an anointing of the Spirit which makes it unnecessary for anyone to instruct the one anointed, as the Spirit teaches everything and it is the truth. This view has been extended in the history of the church and is connected with the concept of conscience. Secondly, the view is present in the New Testament, particularly in Matthew's gospel, that some members of the community have a teaching role which gives them authority

138

to offer moral guidance to their fellow Christians. This dual recognition of external teaching and an internal enlightenment, which influences final choice, remains the orthodox teaching in the Roman Catholic Church to this very day.

Once again it would be far outside the role of this book to trace the rise of the external teaching or magisterium through the centuries and the relevant roles of bishops and theologians. Suffice it to say that gradually, and in particular during the last hundred years, the magisterium has been concentrated in the hands of bishops, and in particular, the Pope, centred at Rome. Gradually the church came to see itself as a 'teaching' church, comprising the hierarchy, and particularly the papacy, and the 'learning' church, containing all the others and of course, particularly, the laity. This view found its culmination in the First Vatican Council which saw the definition of papal infallibility in matters of faith and morals.

Following the First Vatican Council, there has not however been a spate of infallible statements, in fact very few, on matters of faith and none in the area of morality. What there has been is a great deal of papal teaching which, although lacking infallibility, has been very authoritative. This has been the instruction of the 'ordinary' magisterium, as opposed to the 'extraordinary' or infallible teaching.

The Second Vatican Council was aware of this excessive concentration of power in the hands of the Pope and was concerned to situate papal authority in the wider context of all the bishops.

In the Dogmatic Constitution on the church there is clearly a re-emphasis of the importance of the local bishop. 'Bishops are preachers of the faith who lead new disciples to Christ. They are authentic teachers, that is, teachers endowed with the authority of Christ, who preach to the people committed to them the faith they must believe and put into practice.'

The people must obey their bishops:

In matters of faith and morals, the bishops speak in the name of Christ and the faithful are to accept their teaching

139

and adhere to it with a religious assent of soul. This religious submission of will and of mind must be shown in a special way to the authentic teaching authority of the Roman Pontiff, even when he is not speaking ex cathedra (i.e. infallibly).

This is perfectly clear and is the standard text quoted by all who believe that individual bishops, priests or laity are breaking the rules or not being obedient enough. No one is spared. Rome is bombarded with complaints against individual bishops, and bishops receive innumerable letters about laymen including, no doubt, the author of this book. Eminent theologians such as Kung, Schillebeeckx and Curran have all been subjected to investigation, with the results varying according to the prevailing atmosphere in Rome. There is nothing new about such controversy. It has been present since the beginning of the church and will continue until the end of time. It is a necessary process to evaluate truth. What matters is that justice is done in the process of judgment, which unfortunately does not always happen. However, the silenced priest of yesterday is the hero of tomorrow, as happened to many theologians who had their day in the Second Vatican Council, in particular Teilhard de Chardin. But all this refers to theologians: what about lay people?

The Laity

In the course of the history of the church, more and more power was appropriated by the priest, the bishop and, in particular, the Pope. The laity were left with little but to be taught and to obey. This cannot be right and the Second Vatican Council began the necessary correction.

The church as a whole is seen as participating in the priestly, kingly and prophetic characteristics of Christ. The tensions that have unfolded since the council, in promulgating the implications of the laity sharing in these features, and restoring a balance between laity and clergy, hierarchies and Rome, are enormous and continue to this day. The detailed description is a matter for the historian. Only one aspect will be considered here: the question of prophecy. In other words, through whom does the Holy Spirit speak in the life of the church?

The council made it clear that the teaching authority of the bishops is a prophetic activity. But this is not confined to bishops: it includes the laity also:

> Christ, the Great Prophet, who proclaimed the Kingdom of His Father by the Testimony of His life and the power of His words, continually fulfils His prophetic office until his full glory is revealed. He does this not only through the hierarchy who teach in His name and with His authority, but also through the laity.

It is thus inconceivable, after the Second Vatican Council, to think that truth in the church is only to be found in official teaching.

More particularly in the matters that concern this book, that is, sexual matters, I have advocated that in the case of contraception the faithful be consulted. This is not a matter of democracy. It is simply doing what the council suggests; in the section on 'Marriage and Family in the Modern World' it has this to say:

> Redeeming the present time and distinguishing eternal realities from their changing expressions, Christians should actively promote the values of marriage and the family, both by the example of their own lives and by co-operation with other men of good will. Thus, when difficulties arise, Christians will provide, on behalf of family life, those necessities and help which are suitably modern. To this end, the Christian instincts of the faithful, the upright moral consciences of men, and the wisdom and experience of persons versed in the social sciences will have much to contribute.

As far as contraception is concerned, the voice of all other Christians of good will has spoken in favour of it. What remains is that the 'Christian sense of the faithful' be measured, and this sense has been expressed in survey after survey.

The church recognises that it does not have all the answers and it needs the help of all its people. Here is the council again:

> To promote such an exchange, the Church requires special help, particularly in our day, when things are changing very rapidly and the ways of thinking are exceedingly various. She must rely on those who live in the world, are versed in different institutions and specialities and grasp their innermost significance in the eyes of both believers and unbelievers. With the help of the Holy Spirit, it is the task of the entire people of God, especially pastors and theologians, to hear, distinguish and interpret the many voices of our age, and to judge them in the light of the divine Word.

The whole of this book is influenced by my own psychological thinking and, just in case someone thinks this is a quirk of the author, unrelated to the life of the church, let me add another quote: 'In pastoral care, appropriate use must be made not only of theological principles but also of the findings of the secular sciences, especially of psychology and sociology. Thus the faithful can be brought to live the faith in a more thorough and mature way.' I could go on adding quotation after quotation on the role of the laity in the life of the church. Enough has been given. The conclusion is inevitable that the laity have an immense responsibility to play in the life of the church and, if they fail to do so, they would be failing as Catholics.

Discernment

It may be said that all this is very well, and cannot be denied, but differences are bound to remain: someone has to teach, and that someone is the bishop, in particular the bishop of Rome. This is perfectly true. What is even more true, though, is that what is taught must have the marks of discernment.

It must appeal to people's minds and feelings, that is, have the ring of intellectual truth and at the same time feel right, otherwise human beings cannot give their assent. Even this will not always be realised, but the perfect answer is likely to be achieved when the laity are allowed to do what they have been invited to do, which is to make their contribution.

My Position

Finally since I am a dissenter from a number of positions in sexual ethics I owe it to everyone to show how I harmonise my position in remaining a Catholic.

First I should repeat that I believe in moral norms and I shall rejoice on the day Catholic moral theology emerges from its present difficulties and expresses clear views on moral matters, which will have the assent of the majority of Roman Catholics and many other Christians. Christians of other denominations have everything to gain by such a move. In the deliberations of moral theology the laity have a vital and necessary contribution; without this input moral theology will have no validity.

I recognise clearly and unequivocally that, whatever contributions the laity or clergy make, someone has to be the teaching voice in the church. This has to be the bishop as visualised in the Second Vatican Council but not yet fully developed, and the Roman Pontiff, as part of episcopal collegiality. I am equally clear that, if this teaching voice of the church is to receive the assent of the faithful, then what it teaches must have had their discernment. Part of the present difficulties is that what the church teaches on sexual matters has not been party to this discernment, and so its teaching is flouted to a large extent. This worries me extensively because it undermines the authority of the church and, ultimately, the presence of Christ in the world.

I have expressed in this book the view that the church will not lose prestige if it modifies some of its sexual thinking. But I would rather face some loss of status in the eyes of a small minority of people to get the church to the point where its

143

teaching on sexual matters harmonises with the sense of its faithful, and other Christian denominations, so that all can see it teaches with authority. There is a current view in the church that what matters above all is that authority should be seen to exist. I thoroughly disagree with this position. If authority teaches that which the majority of people, or the 'sense of the faithful', see as palpably untrue, then that authority is undermined. It is true that people have a sneaking admiration for persistence, but they have an even greater respect for the truth.

And so what happens to a layman like me, who shares in the vast majority of the teachings on sexual ethics and on the structure of the church that designates teaching to the bishops, but loyally dissents on some matters? The council has the answer.

> An individual layman, by reasons of the knowledge, competence or outstanding ability which he may enjoy, is permitted and sometimes even obliged to express his opinion on things which concern the good of the church. When occasions arise, let this be done through the agencies set up by the church for this purpose. Let it always be done in truth, in courage and in prudence, with reverence and clarity towards those who by reason of their sacred office represent the person of Christ.

This is precisely what I have done in this book and in other writings, although in the course of twenty-five years of writing my main aim has been to promote the Christian faith, especially by using psychology. Besides my writings I have dedicated myself to the prevention of marital breakdown in a variety of ways, but particularly by establishing the Marriage Research Centre at the Central Middlesex Hospital in London.

But I cannot deny that there is inevitable tension which is a source of deep pain. I know through travelling round the world that my personal agony is shared by many. Everyone from the Pope to the last practising layman knows there is a big division in the church on some sexual matters. In the light of this division, what should the dissenting Catholic do?

Clearly every Christian must ultimately obey his conscience, the final arbiter in moral choices. But before doing so every Catholic should be familiar with the teaching, and give serious attention to the case made by the church. I have followed this advice throughout my life, but particularly in what I write and say. I try to give an accurate formulation of the teaching of the church, put forward the arguments on its behalf and then, where I dissent, put forward the other side, and let people make up their own minds. Fortunately, in practice, I devote most of my time to lecturing and working on behalf of the prevention of marital breakdown, which is an area where there can be no equivocation. I long for the day when all teaching on sexual matters can be equally clear.

14

Beyond AIDS:
From Chastity to Sexual Integrity

AIDS is a dreadful disease which at the time of writing is a killer. It is potentially the most serious disease of our age and every care should be taken to avoid infection. In this book the case is made that the campaign waged by governments leaving sexual behaviour unaltered and relying on condoms is ill-conceived. The basic threat is to be found in sexual activity itself which, however well protected, remains dangerous.

The advent of AIDS is therefore an occasion to re-examine the meaning of human sexuality in the light of progress in medicine and the advent of contraception, which between them have made a biological basis for sexual morality obsolete. Infant mortality, which made repeated pregnancies necessary and often caused the death of the mother, and which necessitated new relationships are events of history. Nowadays couples may often achieve the family size they desire through a couple of conceptions; and the overwhelming majority of sexual activity is non-procreative. It has been shown that, while this has produced a fundamentally new ethical situation, a good deal of traditional morality remains. In this last chapter I want to summarise the situation by looking beyond AIDS.

While the closest attention must be paid to sexual conduct in the immediate future, it is inevitable that an answer will be found to AIDS. Even more important will be the restoration of sexual behaviour on a basis of love and not fear. Fear is not a suitable basis for motivating anything human, since it does

146

not lead to a precise attitude. When fear goes old habits
return, which could easily happen when AIDS becomes treat-
able. This will be unfortunate because, as already stated, new
conditions exist in the world which demand a new basis for
sexual morality.

Sexual Integrity

Such sexual morality will not be accomplished by easy
recourse to the traditional term 'chastity', which is associated
with a hostile restriction on sexual pleasure. Instead, what I
am advocating is that we use the term sexual integrity, which
is a concept that applies to everyone, believers and non-
believers. Sexual morality is not a prerogative or an obligation
for Christians alone; everyone has a responsibility to apply
their sexuality in a way that does justice to their humanity.
This integrity starts with the view that human beings are
programmed in childhood to love and, after puberty, towards
sexual attraction, which leads to pairing and the formation
of a bond called marriage, within which love is expressed.

Within this framework, sexual attraction is considered to
be the single most important force in human beings, whose
main purpose is to form and maintain bonds, and secondarily
to continue the race. The main purpose of human sexuality
is then no longer biological but personal, in which love is the
predominant theme; and sexual integrity is related to the
three basic concepts of person, relationship and love.

Sexual integrity is concerned with following the development of persons in relationships, which acquire and express
love. Sexual integrity begins with conception when an act of
love sets a new life in motion: the first responsibility of parents
is to help their children learn what it means to be truly loved.
Sexual integrity will be concerned in the future with the
interaction between parents and children, through which the
essentials of human love are learned. This task is mainly
social and psychological.

After puberty, sexual attraction is concerned with the next
critical development of the personality, the separation of

children from parents and their orientation towards a man or woman outside the family circle. Sexual integrity is now concerned with the interaction of the sexes, mutual exploration, and finally the establishment of pairing. During this period sexual intercourse is inappropriate, for it is not a basic means of assisting the suitability of pairing. Despite the powerful pressure for coitus it is not primarily an act which defines suitability for partnership.

When bonding has been established, then coitus is eminently suited to reinforce the bond. Sexual integrity is concerned with taking every social, physical and psychological care that the physical act becomes an intact channel for this bonding through the expression of love. The biology of reproduction is not a primary consideration in effecting this bond, but the presence and care of the children is a strong force for its maintenance. Seen in this light, sexual integrity seeks to avoid anything that disrupts the bond, such as adultery and marital breakdown, and society should do everything it can to reduce both these events.

This outline is consistent with human evolution and makes sense of the traditional Judaeo-Christian warnings against fornication, adultery and divorce, which form a triad whose avoidance preserves the family, the basic unity of society all over the world.

The advent of contraception has made sexual integrity much harder because it has reinforced a human frailty to wish to participate in coitus in a variety of conditions in which bonding is not central. Within the context of bonding, we have a long way to go to find efficient and satisfactory contraceptives, but their presence is a distinct extension of God's gift to man to subdue creation and reveal more clearly the basic design and purpose of coitus – the assistance of bonding rather than procreation.

In this way we can ultimately understand the mystery of sexuality in God himself. God, in whose image we have been created, does not use sexuality for the purpose of procreation, but in the Trinity sexuality is the basic force of love which sustains an everlasting relationship of dynamic unity between the three Persons of the Trinity while respecting their unique individuality, in the same way that coitus achieves it for the human couple.

Thus, for me, AIDS is an episode in the long history of dialogue between God and man at a time appropriately arrived at when a new basis for sexual morality has to be achieved. This is to be found in sexual integrity, which is a principle that governs human conduct from the time of conception to death. When sexual integrity is observed, it becomes not only an answer to AIDS but goes beyond it as the predominant basis for sexual ethics in the twenty-first century.